DOES ANYONE ELSE FEEL LIKE I DO?

DOES ANYONE ELSE FEEL LIKE I DO?

And Other Questions Women Ask Following an Abortion

PAM KOERBEL

Doubleday

NEW YORK   LONDON   TORONTO   SYDNEY   AUCKLAND

PUBLISHED BY DOUBLEDAY

a division of Bantam Doubleday Dell Publishing Group, Inc.
666 Fifth Avenue, New York, New York 10103

DOUBLEDAY and the portrayal of an anchor
with a dolphin are trademarks of Doubleday,
a division of Bantam Doubleday Dell Publishing Group, Inc.

Some of the names of persons referred to in this book have been
changed to ensure their privacy.

Unless otherwise noted, Scripture quotations are from the *New American
Standard Bible,* copyright © the Lockman Foundation 1960, 1962, 1963,
1968, 1971, 1972, 1973, 1975, 1977. Used by permission. Other
quotations are from the *Holy Bible, New International Version* (NIV),
copyright © 1973, 1978, 1984, International Bible Society, used by
permission of Zondervan Bible Publishers; the *King James Version* (KJV);
and the *Good News Version.*

DESIGNED BY KARIN BATTEN

Library of Congress Cataloging-in-Publication Data

Koerbel, Pam.
   Does anyone else feel like I do? : and other questions women ask
following an abortion / by Pam Koerbel.
      p.   cm.
   Includes bibliographical references
   1. Abortion—Religious aspects—Christianity.   2. Abortion—United
States—Psychological aspects.   I. Title.
HQ767.25.K64   1990
363.4'6—dc20   89-25982
                                                                 CIP

ISBN 0-385-26566-2

Printed in the United States of America

July 1990

FIRST EDITION

BVG

The women quoted on these pages speak for the hundreds of thousands, perhaps millions, who remain silent. As you read their words, remember that each woman quoted is one of us. Often she has found a method of dealing with her grief, living with her loss, and facing her future with confidence and hope. She may still have problems, but she actively seeks solutions. She expects to find answers. You should expect to find them too!

CONTENTS

AUTHOR'S NOTE

Quotes appear frequently throughout this book with a woman's first name, or with first and last names, or anonymously. These quotes are from women who have written voluntarily to share what is on their hearts. Many times women have phrased a thought in such a way that it reached out and touched me and, I trust, will touch you. I believe you will find comfort in the words of another who shares or has shared the same query, pain, or solution. The women quoted on these pages speak for the hundreds of thousands, perhaps millions, who remain silent. As you read their words, remember that each woman quoted is one of us. Often she has found a method of dealing with her grief, living with her loss, and facing her future with confidence and hope. She may still have problems, but she actively seeks solutions. She expects to find answers. You should expect to find them too!

ACKNOWLEDGMENTS

Although space limitations prohibit acknowledging every person by name who supported and encouraged me in this work, I would be remiss not to mention the following: my husband, Leigh, for his sacrificial love and understanding support of my post-abortion work; my children, Michael, Mark, Sarah, and Rebekah, who teach me daily the preciousness of life and who provide joys and challenges beyond measure; my editor, Theresa D'Orsogna, for believing in the need for this book; Mrs. Cheryl Smith for taking time from her busy schedule to critique the manuscript; the hundreds of women who have opened their hearts to me; and those who have permitted me to quote their words in order that others might heal. To each of you—thank you!

INTRODUCTION

You've had an abortion. You thought it would solve your problem. You were wrong. Instead, a whole new set of problems has emerged.

The gnawing guilt, grief, and anxiety won't go away. You ask yourself, "Why, oh why, did I ever do it?" Questions plague your mind as you mull over your abortion. Round and round you go in a self-inflicted, silent hell. Is there any way out?

YES! Others have struggled with the realization that abortion is not the "easy way out" of an untimely pregnancy. Some of them have found satisfactory answers to their emotional trauma.

My first book, *Abortion's Second Victim,* chronicles my personal experience with abortion, delves into the medical, legal, and theological arguments surrounding abortion, and includes practical steps to take in dealing with the basic emotions that get out of kilter following an abortion—emotions such as guilt, anger, grief, depression, and shame.

Hundreds of letters and phone calls have reached me from women across America and from some foreign countries. You have written, oftentimes pouring out your hearts in long, long letters. For the first time you were able to share your thoughts with someone else. I read those letters and cried or rejoiced. Along with your personal stories, you often asked questions—specific questions for which you sought answers. You recognized your need for healing. You wanted help and were willing to apply the answers you found to your life. Many of you have healed well. You have gone on to share answers with others who hurt. However, countless women still struggle with specific questions.

Does Anyone Else Feel Like I Do? offers insights to help you put your abortion experience into perspective and to aid your healing process. Some of my words may hit hard. You may find old wounds aching or new ones exposed. Take heart; wounds usually hurt before they heal. Now the question is— are *you* willing to do what is necessary to put your past behind you and get on with your life?

P.J.K.
1990

"And you shall know the truth,
and the truth shall make you free."

John 8:32

DEDICATION

*This book is dedicated
to my parents,
Carl and Anne Hoffman,
who by their example
have taught me
the meaning of
love and forgiveness.*

DOES ANYONE ELSE
FEEL LIKE I DO?

CHAPTER ONE

How Did This Ever Happen to Me?

"I was very, very confused. My feelings were so mixed. All along I was told it was the right thing to do, but then why was I feeling like it was so wrong and terrible? I hated myself so much. I wanted to scream. I wanted my son or daughter back but it was too late. The nurses wouldn't talk to me. All they would say is 'relax,' or 'it's okay, it's all over now.' "

Anonymous

When we submitted to our abortions, we never dreamed it was not the end but merely the beginning of our problems. Most of us thought we were escaping from an impossible situation. We traded a pregnancy for freedom—or so we thought. Now, in the midst of our tears and pain, we begin to question the cause of our anguish:

- Why was I so stupid?
- Why was I driven by such desperation?
- Why did I say yes to abortion when I meant no?
- Why couldn't I have made another decision?

3

- Why was I too cowardly to stand by the ideals I had always held?
- How could I have done such a terrible thing?
- How did this ever happen to me?

We ask ourselves these questions over and over. Desperately our minds turn them this way and that as we search to give some meaning and reason to the horror in the midst of which we find ourselves. We can hardly believe abortion is a reality in our lives. Yet it is.

Most of us never in our wildest dreams imagined we could ever abort our own unborn babies. In fact, some of us were pro-life prior to our untimely pregnancies. Many of us never gave abortion much thought one way or the other. And to a few, abortion was a matter of choice—an option readily considered and chosen. The truth is that no person knows what he or she will do in a particular situation until faced with the reality of a decision.

Because the questions concerning the beginning of our abortion experience bear so heavily on our minds, first we will briefly explore some of our initial questions. These are the ones that usually surface as we begin to mentally explore our abortions. These questions are our attempts to see if there can be any positive answers to what we have done. Sometimes they are our attempt to escape personal responsibility for our actions. Most often, however, they are honest questions that were never asked *before* our abortions. Knowing the answers will help you to understand why you feel as you now do about your abortion.

What did the abortion do?

We need to explore this question and come to a definite answer. Scientists and medical professionals generally agree that human life begins at conception.[1] From that point on, nothing is added to the new life except time and growth. "Biological data confirms that the life of a newly conceived human embryo is a life belonging to neither the father nor the mother but to a new member of the human race, who will grow up into a fully developed adult if given simple nourishment and protection."[2]

On the legal front, there is also support for the stand that human life begins at conception. On July 3, 1989, the U.S. Supreme Court upheld a Missouri statute, leaving intact that statute's preamble which states that human life begins at conception (Webster vs. Reproductive Health Services).

As further proof that human beings reside in their mothers' wombs prior to birth, technology has advanced to the point that in utero operations are performed on the baby. He or she is recognized as a human being who is alive and treatable. Tort[3] law considers the unborn baby a person. His or her death is considered a crime if it occurs due to an attack on the pregnant woman. In some states the parents have been awarded remuneration for the crime against the unborn child.

Even pro-abortion advocates no longer argue for abortion on the grounds of the viability of the unborn baby or when life begins. The argument used today focuses on a woman's right to do as she pleases with her own body. What pro-abortion advocates never mentioned is that by doing what she wanted (sex), the woman invited a new person to reside within her womb for approximately nine months. The simple

1. See, for example, Dr. Landrum Shettles and David Rorvik, *Rites of Life* (Zondervan Publishing House, Grand Rapids, 1983).
2. Richard Doerflinger, Associate Director for Policy Development, Bishops' Committee for Pro-Life Activities, National Conference of Catholic Bishops, as quoted in *The Washington Times,* Letters to the Editor, February 10, 1989.
3. "In law, a wrongful act, injury, or damage (not involving a breach of contract), for which a civil action can be brought." *Webster's New World Dictionary of the American Language,* college edition (The World Publishing Company, New York, 1966), p. 1538.

fact is that this is how human beings normally begin—in the wombs of their mothers! Nothing we do or say will alter that fact.

God also speaks to the subject of human life living in the womb. Psalms 139:13–16 states, "For Thou didst form my inward parts; Thou didst weave me in my mother's womb. I will give thanks to Thee, for I am fearfully and wonderfully made; Wonderful are Thy works, And my soul knows it very well. My frame was not hidden from Thee, When I was made in secret, and skillfully wrought in the depths of the earth. Thine eyes have seen my unformed substance; And in Thy book they were all written, The days that were ordained for me, When as yet there was not one of them."

Given the natural course of events, once conception occurs and pregnancy begins, a human being will emerge from the womb. Therefore, what the abortion did was to kill the baby that was growing in our womb. Whether or not we realized what was happening, the fact is the action of abortion killed our baby.

And in the killing of our own babies, we have begun a tidal wave. The once tiny ripples have gained force and momentum as they toss us to and fro. Others have become unavoidably caught in the whirling vortex surrounding our abortions. Husbands, parents, siblings, friends—struggling to free themselves from the guilt and hurt and pain of the knowledge that a small, precious life is gone. Irretrievably gone.

How did this happen?

Perhaps we had a lack of the facts regarding our unborn babies. Perhaps we had a lack of faith in facing an unknown future. Hindsight is always twenty-twenty. At the time others may have encouraged us by saying, "It's okay." They may have been trying to help us to do the best thing for us. As for me, although I was informed about the development of unborn babies, I had never actually *seen* a developing baby. At the back of my mind I kept thinking, "It can't be true that this is a baby—elsewise, how could abortion be legal?" Terms like "fetal tissue" and "product of conception" eased my conscience and enforced my decision.

The other side of this coin is that the legality of abortion since 1973 has created a carelessness and promiscuity in America's young women. Approximately 80 percent of abortions are performed on unmarried women. Linda writes, "Yes, it [the abortion] was legal. Not only would I never have consented to an illegal abortion, I doubt I would have ever taken the chance of having sex had I not known in the back of my mind there was a way out." Abortion has become, to many women, an alternate form of birth control.

Most of our abortions were a direct result of selfishness. We live in an I-oriented society—so much so that we aren't consciously aware of the fact because it is a constant pattern of living. *My* rights, *I* want, for *me,* and so forth are the standards by which the majority live. Is it any wonder we got caught up in the pleasure of sex, which in turn led to the inconvenience of pregnancy, which then caused us to choose self over another and have an abortion?

Why wasn't I told the truth?

Once we understand and admit that a baby died when we submitted to an abortion, the angry question rips from us: "Why wasn't I told it was a baby I was aborting?"

There are several reasons why you weren't fully informed. Remember that the abortion industry is a multimillion-dollar business. Like all businesses, it wants to make a profit. How many women do you think would actually go through with an abortion if they understood a baby lived in their wombs?

On the other hand, some people honestly believe they are helping to protect our right to privacy by refusing to fully inform women considering abortion of the physical and emotional risks. To these people, "rights" outweigh the life and well-being of women and their unborn children.

Then there are those people who sincerely wanted to help *you*. Although their efforts were misguided, their primary goal was to help you to do what was best for you. They themselves may not have understood what an abortion is and does.

Finally we must look at ourselves. Is it possible someone did try to tell you the truth? I clearly remember one social worker at the clinic I visited for prenatal care telling me, "Pam, if you have an abortion, you will regret it the rest of your life." Her words return very clearly to me now. Back then I scarcely heard them. Sometimes we don't listen to the facts. We practice selective listening, which causes us to hear only what we *want* to hear. Possibly we heard what eased our conscience rather than the truth that was intermingled with the "easy" words.

Why did I choose abortion?

Although each woman's specific reasons for choosing abortion are unique and personal, most fall into one of several broad categories. Perhaps you were separated or divorced and involved in an affair. Maybe you were single, having casual sex. You wanted no one to know. Stephanie writes, "I couldn't make a better decision because my eyes were focused on me and not on God. I had already gotten pregnant, and Satan had a good hold of me. I only wish there had been someone there to help me make a different decision." Possibly you were made to feel guilty for your desire to remain pregnant. As one woman relates, "First I felt excited and determined not to have an abortion. After talking with [my friend] and the psychologist, I felt like that was selfish on my part. I felt like if I were to keep my baby I would be a [malicious] manipulator trying to get the father into a corner. I felt guilty for wanting to let my baby live." It wasn't that you didn't want your untimely baby, but you were led to believe giving birth would be unfair to you both. Possibly your physical health suggested abortion. In rare instances, pregnancy may have resulted from rape or incest.[4] Fear related to the responsibilities of child rearing may have overwhelmed you. Amanda concludes, "I was young, scared, alone and not financially secure. I felt unable to 'deal' with a baby. I also did not want to cause my family any pain." You may have wanted the baby, but the pregnancy got in the way. You just couldn't see past the nine months to the birth of a baby. You wanted and needed someone to take you by the hand and say, "It will all work out." Selfishness may have been your only motive. Maybe you were married and felt one more child was one too many. Often the legality of abortion helped us make up our minds. "If it's legal, it must be okay." Our reasons are varied, and yet a similar thread weaves them all together. We were involved in a situation where a pregnancy was untimely, a nuisance in our lives—either financially, emotionally, physiologically, or socially. The simple fact is, we wanted to be free—unencumbered with a child—to resume our lives.

And so we aborted our babies, oftentimes not realizing what we had actually done until the act was accomplished and it was too late to turn back. We couldn't know then that we'd feel this way now. If we had, we probably wouldn't have aborted. Situation ethics dictated our actions. Then it seemed okay. Now it seems so wrong (Proverbs 14:12–13). And so an hour, a month, a year, or many years later we begin to ask ourselves, "What have I done?"

What have I done?

"Oh, dear God, what have I done?" The ramifications of this question go further than the act of killing an unborn child.

4. See Dr. and Mrs. J. C. Willke, *Abortion: Questions and Answers,* revised edition (Hayes Publishing Co. Inc., Cincinnati, Ohio, 1985), pp. 146–155.

Our entire being is affected. One reason women were created is to nurture new lives. It is the very essence of our being. Over the past few years outspoken women have tried to convince us motherhood is not something to be desired. These women depict pregnancy and motherhood as a curse placed on us by the nature of our physiology. Our logic said, "True," but now that we have put logic before our hearts, our hearts cry out in pain and brokenness.

Do you know the story of King Solomon and the arguing mothers? Two women lived in the same house. Each gave birth to a baby within days of the other. One child died and the other lived. Both claimed the living child and came before King Solomon for a decision. In God's wisdom, King Solomon decreed the living child should be divided with a sword and one half given to each woman. "Then the woman whose child was the living one spoke to the king, for she was deeply stirred over her son, and said, 'Oh, my lord, give her the living child, and by no means kill him.' But the other said, 'He shall be neither mine nor yours; divide him!' Then the king answered and said, 'Give the first woman the living child, and by no means kill him. She is his mother' " (1 Kings 3:26–27). How did King Solomon know who the mother of the living child was? The true mother was willing to let her son live with the other woman rather than see him die. Her natural instinct was to protect the life of her child at any cost.

What have we done? We've allowed a callous mind-set to overrule our natural instincts. We've permitted logic to rule our hearts. We've allowed our minds to listen and accept lies because we were so desperate to cover up our indiscretion, or to get on with our interrupted lives, or to have things back the way they were prior to our pregnancies.

We have permitted our own flesh and blood to be torn violently from our wombs. It doesn't matter what we were told; the truth became startlingly evident as we viewed the aftermath of our decision. One woman remembers, "When I first saw the completely formed baby in a book a few weeks after my abortion, I think I came as close to having a mental breakdown as I ever have in my life."

Why did God allow this to happen?

As we search for answers, we think of God—admitting, perhaps for the first time, His existence. But we need someone to blame and so we cry out, "Why did God allow this to happen? Surely *He* could have stopped the pregnancy." We need to realize that most actions bring natural consequences without supernatural intervention by God. Sexual intercourse brings the possibility of a new baby being conceived. A woman once commented to me, "If you go out in the rain without an umbrella, you are going to get wet." So it is with sexual intercourse. And even with an "umbrella" we sometimes get "wet." What we need to realize is that God would not put a baby into our wombs for us to kill, for He says in Deuteronomy 30:19, "I call heaven and earth to record this day against you, that I have set before you life and death, blessing and cursing: therefore choose life, that both thou and thy seed may live."

God is omniscient—all-knowing. He knew before you were born that you would one day abort your baby. He didn't want that to happen, but He knew it would. God *could* have kept you from becoming pregnant, but that is not how He chooses to work. God planned the world so that events follow one another naturally according to the choices *we* make. The natural consequences of our actions occurred. We had sex. We became pregnant. We did not choose life for our babies. We chose abortion.

I once met a clinical psychologist who teaches her clients to say, "I am a woman who was not strong enough to say no to abortion." I believe she offers this as a less painful option to admitting one has chosen to have an abortion. However, each of us has it within ourselves to say no in such situations. We may not want to say no. It may be extremely difficult. Yet

11

we do have a free will that can choose to say yes or no. The simple truth is that I chose to abort my unborn baby. *I* chose. *I* made the decision. Oh, to be certain, I had plenty of "help." But *I* was the one who said yes. Misguided, confused, selfish—but the decision in the vast majority of cases was ours. Achnes Smith offers sound advice: "I would just like to stress the point that it is extremely important that women who have aborted face up to the fact that they played an active role in the destruction of their baby. We can't put all the blame on doctors, nurses or family and friends. The decision was ultimately ours, no matter how coerced we might have been. Without acknowledging our [role] in the abortion act, there can never be true reconciliation." And so we must learn to acknowledge and to say, "I chose to abort my unborn baby. I was wrong. Now, what can I do to live with this irreversible decision?"

Why am I just now beginning to hurt?

Psychologists tell us there are several ways our mind uses to permit us to live with our wrong actions when we do not choose to face up to what we have done. Denial is knowing you did something wrong, but refusing to admit it. You may express denial by saying, "I didn't do it," or "I didn't do anything wrong." Suppression is knowing you did something wrong but refusing to consciously think about it. Repression is being unaware of negative feelings. Rationalization is convincing yourself you had no choice. Finally we come to projection: this method of coping with wrong actions involves passing the buck by thinking, "It was someone else's fault." Additionally, there are those people who honestly do not believe they acted wrongly when they had an abortion. My sister tells of attending a party. She was one of ten women present. The topic of abortion arose, and to her horror, my sister discovered she was the only woman present who had *not* had an abortion. "Pam," she told me, "they were discussing their abortions as if they had gone to have a wart removed." Some people have no absolute values in their lives, no definite pattern of right and wrong. To these people, abortion is truly acceptable. That still does not make it right.

Most of us have used one or more of the coping mechanisms just mentioned at one time or another. Which have you used? Did they help? Possibly for a time, but now all the bad feelings have resurfaced or surfaced for the first time, and the pain and guilt and grief just won't go away.

Here we are. We who live to regret our abortions. What are we to do? How do we go about putting our lives back together? How do we pick up the broken pieces and mend them so a complete woman emerges once more? Broken but mended—with a strong glue that will not come undone. You want that, don't you? That is what this book is all about. There *are* answers. I found them. Others have found them. You, too, can find them and make them work for you.

If you have come to the point in your life where you are able to admit you killed an unborn human being when you had your abortion—if you can say, "I killed my unborn baby; I was wrong"—then you have taken the first step in the healing process. Keep walking—you'll make it!

CHAPTER TWO

Does Anyone Else Feel Like I Do?

"Of course they do—but at the time of my abortion I didn't know anybody else who had already had an abortion so I didn't have anyone to compare my feelings with."

Debra

Many women wonder if their feelings are unique. The life of an aborted woman is one of the loneliest on earth. In spite of the evidence, you may find it difficult to believe that anyone else could have actually *done* what you did. You can't believe anyone else *feels* as you do. Most of all, you can't believe anyone could understand, love, or forgive you, a baby killer. It is vital to know that you are not alone in your feelings concerning your abortion. Read the quotes from letters I have received. You will see that others do feel as you do, some worse, some not as bad. But the truth is that *most* women have some negative feelings following an abortion.

If abortion is recognized as legal, why do I feel like such a criminal? (From a questionnaire)

I was unable to cope with what I had done in any way except to deny that I had any other alternative. I repeated the "comfort" of other people to myself, "It was for the best." Once I came to the realization that I had killed my own unborn baby (a child that was as human and unique as myself or anyone else), I went through a time of deep guilt and depression. (Anonymous)

My immediate response was relief—but that soon passed away and all that I have ever felt since is guilt. I knew that abortion is killing and I would give anything to have the child now. (Anonymous)

I always thought I was the only woman who didn't want to abort her baby but did anyway. It is comforting to know I'm not a freak. (Hollie)

Why do I think it futile (when I think of the 4,000 plus women who put themselves through the Procedure every day) to ever see an end to this. I am one of so many and my decision has profoundly changed my life, so why do I feel so uncomforted when I tell my good friends about it and they just shrug their shoulders and say, "Yeah, I know lots of girls that did it and they're still nice people." (Anonymous)

The feeling I had after the abortion was like a cancer eating away at me every day. At the time of the abortion I didn't tell any family members because I was so afraid it would hurt them, and I just didn't want to be a disappointment to them. But the more I didn't talk about it the more it ate away at me, like I was hiding something and didn't want to. (Anonymous)

For me it was wrong because killing my babies was against all that I believed in and knew, instinctively and intellectually. I also believe that God's Holy Spirit was working to bring me to repentance, which is why I suffered extreme guilt. I wish I had thought about how I would feel afterward, before I did it. (Regina)

Most women can at least say they acted in ignorance of God's law, but I knew better. Yet I still did it. Now I wrestle with the fact that my pride is what has harmed me, and even still, I am mortified by my deed—yet have to ask myself if it is because I failed or because I wounded the heart of God and transgressed his laws. (Kate)

The baby is a human life, and the suffering and guilt I've experienced are not the result of an *acceptable* action. (Judy Bates)

[I feel] anger that abortion is happening in our nation and world. Anger over the deception and apathy of most people. Not blaming them, however, I was once deceived as they are. Grief and sadness over the above. For myself, I feel regret or deep remorse that I can't change what I did to my child. (Anonymous)

I don't discuss it, but I always read about it. As if subconsciously I know I don't deserve to have one day's peace for being so deceived by Satan! (Anonymous)

As a result of my abortion I spent the next nine years trying to understand and cope with all the mixed up feelings of guilt and shame. . . . My marriage was all but over [but] to the world outside I was strong and could cope with everything life threw at me. (Christine)

The doctor that did my pregnancy test had a lot to do with my decision without him realizing. When he came back in with a positive on the test, he asked me in a real disgusted tone, "Well, what are you going to do now!" I felt so cheap and dirty. I didn't want anyone else to know how cheap and dirty I was. (Anonymous)

16

The main feeling is that I am alone. Nobody knows about it, in fact, I lied to friends and family as to why I kept getting sick. (A nineteen-year-old)

I chose to abort my baby in January of 1980. I was seventeen years old. The tremendous guilt and sense of loss that I have felt since then have, at times, been insurmountable. I tried, for nearly five years, to justify my decision to abort. "I was too young," "I was going to college in the fall," "Where would I be now if I had a baby," etc. I came up with all the *really good* excuses—but none of them eased the turmoil that was inside me. (Judy Schmid)

I was very upset and depressed. And I suppose shocked at the horror of what I had just done. The [staff at the clinic] treated it like a daily occurrence, which it was for them. But that procedure, which took maybe fifteen minutes, has affected my life ever since. (Anonymous)

If only I would have been informed of my other options, he or she would be here with me right now. I was young, yes, and with a baby comes much responsibility, and that even means giving up a lot. But I wanted to. That was my child they took from me. They treated "him" as if he were nothing, as if he was trash. But he wasn't, he was my baby, he was alive, he was breathing, he felt pain, he was innocent! If only I could tell him how sorry I am. For others it is part of the forgotten past, but for me, he is still here with me today, not alive, but in my heart. I may never get to hold him, rock him, sing him to sleep, wipe his tears, chase away his fear, but I love him as much today as yesterday. (Anonymous)

Why does no one regret the death of my child but me?

There are people in my life who know about my abortion and yet show no regret, no sympathy, no feelings whatsoever. It hurts when someone you love very much reacts this way. But it happens. I have learned to accept it and go on.

Sometimes it only *seems* as if you alone regret your abortion. There are people who would regret the death of your child if they knew about it. Be assured many people regret the death of your child, but you may not know them or that they hurt with you and for you.

It touches my heart to know that God regrets my child's death. Psalms 56:8 tells us that when we cry, God puts our tears in a bottle. What a lovely picture of someone remembering our hurts!

Does the medical profession recognize my pain?

Investigations have begun into the post-abortion problems women face. America is slowly waking up to the fact that abortion does not set a woman free. Instead abortion accentuates existing problems while at the same time creating new ones. The former surgeon general, Dr. C. Everett Koop, has recommended that new post-abortion studies be conducted. However, as of this writing, groups such as the American Psychological Association and the American Medical Association have refused to recognize the seriousness of abortion's aftermath for women.

What are possible physical side effects from an abortion?

Physical complications resulting from an abortion vary from woman to woman. Complications include incomplete expulsion of placenta or baby, perforated uterus, chronic and acute infections, excessive bleeding requiring blood transfusions, shock, intense pain, damage to other organs, miscarriages, tubal pregnancies, infertility, and death.[1]

What is post-abortion syndrome?

Post-abortion syndrome (PAS) is one term used to describe adverse emotional reactions which occur following an abortion. The following symptoms may occur anywhere from a few hours to many years after an abortion: guilt, anxiety, denial, repression, psychological numbing, depression, regret or remorse, flashbacks, grief, anger, changes in relationships, sexual disorders, avoidance behavior, suicide attempts, survival guilt, sudden crying episodes, surprise at intensity of reaction, feelings of helplessness or powerlessness, lowered self-concept, nightmares, hyperalertness, preoccupation with becoming pregnant again, fear of infertility, bonding problems with subsequent pregnancies and/or other children, disturbed sleep patterns, eating disorders, alcohol and/or substance abuse, anniversary syndrome, phantom child syndrome, and brief psychosis.[2] That's some list! Not all women experience all reactions. And not all women have severe reactions.

Why aren't the complications following an abortion better documented?

Better documentation requires that aborted women complain about their complications. David Reardon sets out six reasons women keep silent:

1. For statistics, see Willke, *Abortion: Questions and Answers,* pp. 104–120.
2. For an explanation of the listed symptoms see Teri and Dr. Paul Reisser, *Help for the Post-abortion Woman* (Zondervan Publishing House, Grand Rapids, 1989), pp. 41–52.

1. Many women have tried to tell others, but find themselves ignored or turned away as "exceptions."
2. Most women sign consent forms prior to an abortion, which imply a woman has no recourse if complications occur.
3. Abortion is usually a family or personal secret. Secrecy and shame compel victims to remain silent about their complications.
4. With regard to long-term complications, women can't be absolutely sure their problems relate to the original abortion.
5. Many women view complications resulting from an abortion as punishment they "deserve" because they had an abortion. Thus they keep silent about both their sin and its complications.
6. Statistics are kept and controlled by the abortionists. "In other words, the party which suffers least, and indeed has the most to gain, also has complete control of the information."[3]

Why do some women not hurt?

I sometimes receive letters such as the following: "All women I know who have had abortions DO NOT regret it. One [woman] has had two [abortions], another five. They brag about it. I feel such pity for them because after my one [abortion] I can see that [these women's] hearts are hard, cold and unfeeling."

In her book, *Helping Women Recover from Abortion,* Nancy Michels states:

. . . many women won't allow themselves to grieve over their aborted child. In order for them to agree to

3. David C. Reardon, *Aborted Women—Silent No More* (Good News Publishers, Crossway Books, Westchester, Illinois, 1988), pp. 108–9.

the abortion, they have convinced themselves that they aren't aborting a child, only a potential life. Therefore, there is nothing to grieve about. In addition, their doctor, and other people who may know about the abortion, will very likely have told them that abortion is merely a medical procedure to correct a mistake. So any symptoms of grief that arise must be ignored by the woman if she is to continue believing she did the right thing by choosing abortion.[4]

However, I receive many letters from women who have had several abortions and finally feel anguish over their actions. Wendy writes, "I remember feeling so free after the first, I hadn't felt that good in a long time. I used these feelings to confirm and justify my actions. With the second I felt relief." She writes for several more pages, relating that her abortions were done out of fear, that she suffered a nervous breakdown, and that she became dependent on drugs. Although she managed to escape hurt for several years, her suffering, once begun, was intense.

Many women camouflage their hurt. They may do this by speaking flippantly of their abortions in an attempt to negate the horror they feel inside. They may remain silent, but inside they're crying. You'd be surprised to discover that women you know—possibly your best friend, sister, or mother—have had abortions and are hurting. Until recently abortion's aftermath has often been ignored or dismissed as a response "religious" women would be expected to have. There are two reasons for this. First, pro-abortionists don't want women to know an abortion produces emotional trauma. Second, we aborted women have largely kept silent about our feelings because of guilt and shame.

On the other hand, some women *have* never hurt from their abortions. These are the women who have aborted, not

4. Nancy Michels, *Helping Women Recover from Abortion* (Bethany House Publishers, Minneapolis, 1988), p. 49.

out of necessity, but from purely selfish desires. They already had enough children, the baby was the wrong sex, their career could not be put on hold, their body would be "ugly" for nine months, and so forth. These women are so busy looking at themselves that they fail to notice a child died. They may *never* recognize what they have done. If they do, they may handle it better than most because these people are task-oriented rather than people-oriented.[5]

Nancy Michels sums the answer up well: "Women who are less likely to be affected by PAS [post-abortion syndrome] are those who rely heavily on rationalizing their actions. That is, they rely more on their thinking than on their feelings. Denial is part of their personality. . . . As long as they can maintain their system of rationalization, they will not likely be affected. But later losses . . . may generate the need to grieve that will arouse the past abortion loss and force the woman to face the unresolved grief."[6]

Do religious beliefs influence a woman's reaction to her abortion?

For years pro-abortion advocates have tried to blame religious beliefs for the guilt women feel following an abortion. Naturally, a religious woman would feel guilty once she realized she had killed her unborn baby. However, Dr. Vincent Rue states, "A growing body of evidence supports the contention that *abortion has a painful aftermath, regardless of the woman's religious beliefs, or how positive she may have felt beforehand about her decision to abort.*"[7] Dr. Anne Speckhard, in her study *Psycho-social Aspects of Stress Following Abortion,* found that

5. Reardon, *Aborted Women—Silent No More,* p. 140.
6. Michels, *Helping Women Recover from Abortion,* p. 38.
7. Dr. Vincent M. Rue, "Post-abortion Syndrome: Sham or Emerging Crisis?" *National Right to Life News,* January 15, 1987.

72 percent of the women questioned reported no identifiable religious beliefs at the time of their abortion.[8]

Then, too, many women have become Christians subsequent to their abortions. At the time of the abortion, these women had no qualms about what they did. Now, faced with their newly found faith in God, these women realize for the first time that their abortion killed their own unborn baby.

I have found that while religious beliefs do not necessarily play a role in determining whether or not a woman has an abortion, a woman's abortion deeply affects her religious beliefs.

What questions do other women want answered?

As part of my research for this book, I sent letters to one hundred women requesting them to list specific questions for which they sought answers following their abortions. Two hundred sixty-six questions were submitted by women responding to this survey. The primary focus of the questions was on self (234), with a few (32) concerning help for others. More women asked about forgiveness (53 questions) than any other topic. Of these questions, 19 focused on forgiveness of self; 18 asked about forgiving others; and 16 concerned God's forgiveness of aborted women. The remaining questions break down as follows:

- Whether complete healing is possible—42
- Pertaining to the aborted baby—30
- Advisability of telling others—26
- Aspects of grieving—17
- Sexual problems—16
- Having more children—15

8. Dr. Anne Speckhard, summary sheet of *Psycho-social Aspects of Stress Following Abortion,* prepared by the Christian Action Council, Falls Church, Virginia, n.d.

- How to tell others—10
- Effect of abortion on childrearing—10
- Helping others to avoid abortion—10
- Why abortion chosen—8
- Self-worth—7
- Why lied to about abortion—6
- Uncategorized questions—16

In selecting specific questions for use in this book, the challenge became which to include from the hundreds of questions I've received, both from the survey I conducted and from unsolicited letters and calls. The questions are as varied and unique as the women who have asked them. Some were specific to the point of requiring a personal letter in response.

Because the questions are interrelated, grouping by broad topics has not been done. Rather, I ordered the questions according to logical mental progression, that is, how you might think through things, from first questions concerning why you consented to an abortion to how you can help others once you are healed. In answering the questions, I speak to you from my heart rather than from a textbook.

Does anyone else feel like you do? You bet they do! Some may have more or fewer symptoms than you, but hundreds of thousands, possibly millions, of women hurt because they aborted their unborn children. Lest you read this chapter and find yourself in total despair, please know that the majority of the women quoted have resolved their abortions and are now living full and happy lives.

CHAPTER THREE

Is It Okay to Cry?

"I cried and cried for days, which now I am aware that I was doing the grieving I had never allowed myself to do for twelve years. You can imagine how that must have been after holding it in that long!"
Paulette Hawkins

Do you ever cry over a sad movie? Do you cry when someone's experience touches your heart? Do you cry when a passage in a book moves you deeply? Do you cry when you are sad? Our emotions usually produce normal, healthy responses to situations which touch our lives—we laugh, shout, cringe, cry.

Yet in the area of abortion, women often find it difficult to shed tears. Although we may *feel* like crying, we often hold those tears inside as we stoically face a less than happy life. Why do we not cry when we feel like crying? I think that most of us feeling remorse from our abortions feel guilty about our feelings. That's an awkward way of saying we don't think we have the right to cry. "After all," we tell ourselves, "abortion is legal, it's accepted, it's the right thing to do. Now that I've gone ahead and done the 'right thing' I have these terrible feelings of remorse. That can't be right. I must let no one know my abortion has affected me so adversely. What will people think? Only a crazy person would feel this way after having done something that is supposed to be right."

Supposed to be right. There is the key. We know deep in our being that what we did was not right. It doesn't matter how much we were *told* it was right. We know we did a terrible thing. Even though we might not yet fully understand why we feel so bad, still a small voice inside of us says, "I am sad. I want to grieve."

Would you cry if you suffered a miscarriage? Would you cry if your child was injured or, worse, had died? Yes. Mourning in these circumstances is considered normal. Indeed, *not* to cry would be the less understood action. We tend to cry when our emotions tell us to mourn. It is only in this area of abortion that we tend to deny our true feelings in an attempt to do what we believe is expected of us. As Kate asks, "When I listen to women (and men) cope with the grief of losing a child by miscarriage or stillbirth, I want to receive the help, but I feel like my grief is illegitimate—almost like I have no right to grieve for my baby. Do I?"

Your abortion has caused great grief because your child, unborn, perhaps unformed, died. Grief is natural when we lose a child. The problem is that abortion is accepted by society, and therefore when we experience grief, we feel guilt and confusion at that natural emotion because it wasn't supposed to be that way. Debbie K. Weiser expresses her feelings following her abortion: "I grieved for my lost baby but I had to push it down and out of my mind because I was the cause of my baby's death."

What is abnormal is *not* to grieve—to hold it inside, to ignore your normal emotions.

How does grief manifest itself?

First, let's consider the basic feelings we have. Here are listed dictionary definitions of the common "sad" feelings about our abortions.

- **Sad:** "Having, expressing, or showing low spirits or sorrow; unhappy; mournful; sorrowful."
- **Mourn:** "To feel or express sorrow; lament; grieve."
- **Regret:** "Sorrow or remorse over something that has happened, especially over something that one has done or left undone."
- **Remorse:** "A deep torturing sense of guilt felt for one's actions."
- **Grief:** "Intense emotional suffering caused by loss, disaster, misfortune, etc.; acute sorrow; deep sadness."[1]

Where do you find yourself in these definitions? Are you merely saddened by your abortion? Do you go a step further and regret your action of abortion? Possibly you suffer from remorse. Grief comes when we are more than saddened by actions done to or by ourselves. Grief causes emotional suffering that can debilitate us. That debilitation can be temporary or long-lasting, depending upon how we respond to our grief.

In order to better understand our turbulent emotions, let's look at the grieving process. Grieving involves more than crying for your lost child. Actually, the grieving process has several stages to it. Generally accepted steps of grieving with regard to abortion include relief, denial, anger, bargaining, depression, and acceptance. Let's look at each step briefly and

1. *Webster's New World Dictionary of the American Language,* college edition (The World Publishing Company, New York, 1966), pp. 637, 962, 1225, 1231, 1282.

determine what occurs and where you are in the grieving process.

Relief is that initial feeling of having a particular action over and done with. It doesn't consider whether the action was right or wrong, merely that it is finally accomplished. "WHEW! I did it. It's done. It's over with." As the reality of our abortion sets in, relief often gives way to denial.

Denial is much easier than facing the guilt we feel. A woman in denial might say something such as "I didn't do anything wrong," or "My awful feelings are false because abortion is legal and must be okay to do," or "I only terminated a pregnancy," or "It was the right decision at *that* time."

At the moment of my own abortion, way in the back of my mind, relief flickered for a moment—the decision had been reached and carried out. Relief gave way to guilt, which quickly changed to denial that I had done anything wrong. Pro-abortion phrases such as "It's my body!" became my motto. My denial did not include refusal to believe a baby had died (as with some women) because my abortion was done at twenty-three weeks with a vaginal delivery. I saw the "blob of tissue" with his ten perfectly formed fingers and ten perfectly formed toes. I could never deny I had killed my own son—only that it had been wrong to do so.

Linda Cochrane writes, "Until women have passed through the denial stage, it is difficult for them to understand their responses to their loss. After the denial stage is passed, then things tend to fall into place and they understand more that the nature of their reaction is in relation to the emotional response to the loss of their child."[2]

Bargaining is thinking or sometimes verbalizing, "If you do this, then I'll do this." For instance, "If you heal me, God, then I will love you," or "I'll forgive my parents [or

2. Linda Cochrane, *Women in Ramah: A Post Abortion Bible Study* (PACE, Falls Church, Virginia, 1986), p. 15. PACE is a ministry of the Christian Action Council Education and Ministries Fund.

28

boyfriend] if they tell me they are sorry for convincing me to have an abortion." Bargaining refuses to give unless something is received in return.

Anger is that emotion which lashes out at others and/or festers inside of us, depending on our response to those who have hurt us, or whom we believe have hurt us. Anger can destroy relationships, people, things, and us. However, not all anger is wrong or harmful. When released under control it can prove beneficial. I'll discuss this in greater detail in Chapter Eleven.

Depression occurs when we turn our eyes inward and focus on our situation. It begins with the "woe is me" pity party we indulge in from time to time. See Chapter Ten for a discussion on depression.

Acceptance is admitting we feel remorse for a particular action and then doing the appropriate response of forgiving others and ourselves and accepting God's forgiveness. When you reach the point of acceptance, your healing will be complete.

Why is mourning beneficial?

Mourning is beneficial because it allows you to release pent-up emotions, to clean your internal house, if you will, to clear the air. Mourning allows you to express your emotions in a natural way. Women tend to be more emotional than men. When something touches us, we cry. Grieving goes beyond crying to a pouring out of turbulent emotions over something for which we feel great remorse. It is good to feel great remorse over your abortion. You have lost a child. You carried your child in your womb for six weeks, three months, six months, or longer. That baby was literally formed from your flesh. Not only that, but you were your baby's sole means of protection from the world that he was not yet ready to enter. A unique human being totally dependent on you, his mother, suddenly and with finality gone. That you were instrumental in the death of your child is not the primary focus here. You are sorry the child is gone. Mourn for the dead child, not for your own self. The *child* must be the focus of your grief. That child you never knew, never held, never loved. You need to mourn your baby's death. If you don't, the result will be incomplete healing.

Why is mourning an aborted baby so difficult?

You may encounter difficulties with mourning an aborted baby for one or more of the following reasons:

- You have no memories of experiences with the child.
- Your part in the death of the child causes guilt.
- Society does not equate your loss with the death of a baby.
- Because of shame, guilt, or fear, you may refrain from sharing your grief.
- There is no support from others through the grieving process (i.e., sympathy and condolences are absent).

All these contribute negatively to your realization and acceptance that a baby died during the abortion procedure. With a stillbirth, you can hold the baby, name and bury him. It's not easy to mourn a baby you never knew and never even held in your arms.

How can I mourn?

Women have found various methods to express their grief over the loss of a child to abortion. Several women have sent me poems.

You need not be a poet to write a poem mourning the loss of your child. You will be surprised at how words may flow from your mind through your pen as you allow your heart to release its pent-up emotions. As you write, the words provide a soothing effect. Not only have you expressed your sorrow, you have also left a written record of your feelings.

Another way I encourage women to work through the grieving process is to write out their abortion experience. Many women have written to me—pages and pages telling how they became pregnant, why they aborted, what it was like, how they felt, and/or why they are sad. At the end they usually say something like "Writing . . . helped so much because I felt like I was talking to someone who understood me and didn't condemn my actions or my feelings" (Renée Cochlin).

Even if you have no person to write to, you can still write your feelings down on paper. Pour out your heart through your pen. There is Someone who knows all about the way you feel, who feels the same grief you do over the loss of your child. That someone is God. He will see your words and will understand.

Many of you have told no one about your abortion experience. When you finish writing, tear up your letter or burn it. No one but you and God need see it. The important thing is to get your feelings out of you—to release them in a healthy manner.

Have you ever thought of singing as a means of expressing your grief? Make up your own words and sing your heart out.

Perhaps you feel more comfortable expressing yourself visually rather than with words. Draw, paint, or sculpt as you allow your hands to express your feelings of grief and remorse.

The most obvious method of mourning is to cry. You know that, when you have cried over sorrowful events in your life, a tremendous feeling of release comes just from having let it out. That's what crying is—a release. A healthy and normal release of emotions. Don't be afraid to cry. If you have someone whose shoulder you can literally cry on, go ahead. If you don't, cry alone. But let it out! It's okay to cry!

Who can help me to grieve?

Sometimes the tears just won't come. We need a little help in releasing them. Is there someone in whom you could confide? Someone to whom you could talk? We'll discuss in a later chapter possibilities of people to confide in, but for now, if you know of someone whom you trust, why not tell that person your story? Talking about it in an honest way may begin those tears. Then, don't feel awkward about crying—let it out!

How long should mourning last?

Mourning is good, but there comes a time when we must put off the mourning and resume our lives. Although changed by the death of our baby, we come to realize he[3] would want us to continue forward, to grow wiser and stronger and more determined that abortion will not happen again in our lives.

The length of your grieving depends largely on your desire and willingness to put your abortion to rest. Women frequently write and ask me to caution others to "be patient—it takes time to work through an abortion."

What if I cry unexpectedly?

This is a valid question and one that needs answering. There were times, in the earlier stages of my healing process, that I would discover, to my horror, that I had tears in my eyes at awkward moments. Perhaps I had just read something about abortion, or heard a news broadcast, or listened to a sermon

3. For purposes of continuity with my first book, *Abortion's Second Victim,* I will refer to the aborted baby as "he."

in church. Perhaps I was in a group of women and the topic of abortion came up. WHEW! Was I embarrassed. How could I explain those tears? What would people think? Would they guess I had had an abortion?

Let's explore the options. You could excuse yourself from the room as soon as possible. You could think up a quick reason for the tears. You might laugh and say, "I have something in my eye." You could stifle the tears and hope no one else noticed. You could openly cry and let people think what they may. Or you could speak up and admit why you are crying. No option works all the time. Each situation is different. I often tried to stifle my tears. As I look back, I'm sure people wondered about me. After all, the topic *was* abortion. I've found the best way for me to cope with unexpected tears was to admit that I'd had an abortion. Then my tears could flow naturally.

When I speak publicly, I invariably shed some tears. At one point during the writing of *Abortion's Second Victim,* I began crying so profusely that I called a friend and said, "I can't write this book, it's tearing me apart."

My wise friend said, "Pam, you aren't crying for yourself any longer, you're crying for the millions who have yet to find the healing they desire." One day your tears, too, will come not for your own grief, but for the millions of women who still need to learn that grieving is okay.

CHAPTER FOUR

Why Can't I Forget?

"I don't think about it daily anymore but I probably won't be able to 'forget' about it until abortion is made illegal again so it isn't an issue anymore."

Debra

Do questions such as the following plague your mind?

- Will I ever be able to get through a December without thinking, "My baby would be four years old," "My baby would be five years old," and so on?
- Why do I get totally depressed sometimes and then other times I'll be just fine?
- When will I stop missing my children I never knew?
- How long does it take before I stop thinking about abortion daily?
- Will I ever stop crying in late June (which is when the baby

might have been born) or in late October (when I had the abortion)?

- Can I live with the memories?
- When will I stop thinking about it?

Many women seldom think about their abortions. Then the anniversary date of the abortion or the anticipated birth date of the baby appears on the calendar. The woman begins to feel bad. Depression sets in. She may not even know the cause—yet her subconscious remembers.

My own abortion took place on Valentine's Day 1971. On Valentine's Day 1972, one year following my abortion, I became absolutely hysterical when Leigh (who was then my fiancé) failed to recognize the day with a special gift. Prior to that time I had not cared one way or the other if Valentine's Day passed uneventfully. Finding myself so upset, I thought it was because I was engaged to be married and wanted to feel loved. I *did* want to feel loved. But I'd interpreted the reason for my hysteria incorrectly. Many years later I realized February 14 was the anniversary date of my abortion. I have not had a similar feeling since that first anniversary of my abortion. In fact, as I am working on this book and February 14 has just passed, it amazes me that I should be able to cross such a hurdle without dwelling on the traumatic event which took place on that date many years ago. Today I remember with sadness but realize I can go on.

Why didn't the clinic prepare me for the psychological effects to follow—flashbacks, hallucinations, nightmares, and the like?

The obvious answers to this question are that the personnel at the clinic probably were unaware of or refused to believe abortion produces psychological aftermath. Also, had the clinic told you of such possible occurrences, you probably would have chosen not to abort your baby. That would be bad for business. But let's go a step further and explore the reason *why* you have these symptoms.

Your mind may be focusing on your abortion because of unreconciled emotional trauma related to it. Perhaps you are still experiencing guilt, denial, anxiety, anger, fear, or doubt. Something is wrong and your mind is prompting you to take action to correct the problem.

Shortly following my marriage, I began to dream regularly of babies floating down drains or being pickled in jars. The horrible scenes of my dreams were in vivid color. Leigh often held me in his arms for hours after I awoke in a cold sweat from a dream. During my waking hours my mind flashed back to seeing my aborted baby lying dead between my legs after I delivered him—perfectly formed and horribly burned from the saline. I wanted to die in order to rid myself of the torment. I did not consciously call up these nightmares and flashbacks. They came unbidden and unwelcome. They signaled, "DANGER! Something is wrong." Once I understood how to deal with them and took the appropriate actions, they ceased and have never returned.

Cheryl offers these thoughts: "For some time after my confession I was haunted by the thought that if I could go back, I would abort that baby again because if I had borne that child, I would never have met my husband. The Lord helped me resolve this. . . . He helped me realize it is sinful to ask yourself 'if' questions about the past. I no longer believe this about myself because I am stronger in my faith and further along in my walk with the Lord."

What does it mean to "forget"?

Forgetting doesn't mean not remembering. I have "forgotten" my abortion in the sense that I can write and speak on the topic of abortion without guilt or grief, without anger or bitterness. Forgetting involves refusing to dwell on the act, refusing to rehash it again and again as a method of self-torture. Forgetting is continuing on with your life without remaining emotionally crippled by your loss.

God tells us that if we repent, He will forget our sins. Isaiah 43:25 reads, "I, even I, am the one who wipes out your transgressions for my own sake; And I will not remember your sins." God, being who He is, can never blot out from His mind something which has occurred. But He refuses to call it up and charge it to our account.

I feel a kinship to the apostle Paul. This great man of God had terrible sin in his life. He was a Jewish religious leader who persecuted and tortured Christians prior to his conversion to Christianity. After recounting his life in Philippians 3:4–10, Paul continues in verses 13–15 by informing us that he now lived his life "forgetting what lies behind and reaching forward to what lies ahead." Is Paul contradicting himself? No, I believe Paul wrote these verses to encourage us that although we have committed sins in our life which we will never forget, we can refuse to dwell on them and move forward in our lives. It may not happen overnight. "Forgetting" begins by consciously refusing to dwell on your abortion. Others have forgotten. So can you!

When will I stop thinking about it?

I'm going to share something that happened to me last Sunday during church. Abortion was the furthest thing from my mind as seventeen children were brought forward by their parents to be dedicated to the Lord. Suddenly, there I sat in the midst of five hundred people bawling my eyes out as my mind remembered I have one child I can never physically dedicate to God. At first this rush of emotion baffled me, because I *know* I am healed. Then I realized being healed doesn't mean I will never remember my abortion, only that I have learned to live with it. I'm thankful that embarrassing incident happened, because it's good, occasionally, to remember. It keeps me compassionate toward others who hurt.

Liz writes, "I still have a little trouble on the anniversary of the time of the abortion. . . . And I've had trouble near the time that baby would have been born. But both are getting easier. And I don't think I'm supposed to forget. Just to learn from this and be stronger in my faith."

Why does my abortion continue to plague my thoughts?

Sometimes we aren't able to forget our abortion because we actually *try* to remember the horror of it all. We don't want to forget. We may believe that by calling up our abortion experience, we keep the baby alive. Or we may use remembering as an attempt to punish ourselves.

If you can't forget, it may be a signal that something needs to be resolved. I wish you would take a minute to read Job 11:14–20. How wonderful to know that if we put away our sin, we shall shine as the morning, forget our misery, and experience peace through hope.

Your particular memory will keep returning until the problem is settled. Perhaps you haven't yet grieved for your baby. Maybe you haven't asked God's forgiveness for your abortion. Possibly you are still involved in sexual immorality. Do you still harbor anger or bitterness against someone involved with your abortion? You won't "forget" until you resolve the conflict within your mind. You can't resolve the conflict within your mind until your conscience is clear. Only God can provide a clear conscience. You might want to pray David's prayer for cleansing in Psalms 139:23–24: "Search me, O God, and know my heart; try me, and know my thoughts: And see if there be any wicked way in me, and lead me in the everlasting way" (KJV).

I trust one day this woman's words will be true of you: "I have resolved a lot of my emotions pertaining to my abortion so well through Christ, that I can't remember how I used to feel."

CHAPTER FIVE

Whom Can I Talk To?

"I have always had the need to talk, but no one would talk about it. It has always been a hush-hush topic. But I need to talk about it. . . . it's been kept inside me for four long years."

Anonymous

Talking to someone is different from telling others about your abortion. We *talk to* someone for the purpose of working through our predicaments. Perhaps a better term would be "discuss with." On the other hand, we *tell others* about our experience in order to help *them*. This chapter focuses on talking as differentiated from telling.

Why can't I talk to anyone about this experience?

Often our desire to talk is great, but our fear of exposure and rejection is greater. Our pride tends to get in the way as we wonder, "Will people think less of me? Laugh at me? Hate me?" Sometimes the pain is so great it seems impossible to speak of it openly. Another consideration is that once your abortion is spoken of, you will have admitted how wrong it was. Then you will have to deal with it. You will be unable to hide behind the shield of denial any longer.

Is there any benefit in talking to someone about my abortion?

For a woman who has submitted to an abortion, the desire to talk can be unbearable. You need to share your feelings, to sort it all out verbally. Yet fear or shame or embarrassment keeps you from vocalizing your thoughts. On the other hand, keeping it inside isn't helping. Sometimes you need to have someone put their arms around you. Sometimes the verbal reassurance "It's okay, we'll work through this together" is what you seek. The desire to know that someone still loves them in spite of what they have done prompts some women to break their silence. Other times advice or counsel is desired.

How can I evaluate a post-abortion counselor or support group?

Because abortion is a critical issue in our nation and world today, "help" seems to be cropping up all over the place. A few people and organizations will be out to take your money or exploit you. Thankfully, most have a sincere desire to help you resolve your conflicts (although this does not always guarantee beneficial methods of resolving your problems will be offered).

Here are five practical guidelines to follow when you

decide to talk to someone. If you stick to them, you will more than likely find a sympathetic ear and helping hands.

1. *Choose someone you can trust.* Nothing is worse than telling another person your secret only to have that person blab it all over town. Know the person in whom you choose to confide, or else get a referral from people you trust.

2. *Find someone who will not minimize your abortion experience.* I've heard from several women whose counselors ignored or negated their abortion experience. One woman told her therapist she had had an abortion. The therapist answered, "That's okay, I had one too," and went on to another topic. My friend, your abortion has changed your life. It plays a vital part in how you react and respond to other people and situations. If your counselor, whoever he or she may be, will not permit you to discuss your abortion and your feelings related to it, find another counselor. Don't minimize your feelings about your abortion, and don't permit anyone else to minimize them either.

3. *Choose someone who will give more than a listening ear.* I recently heard an analogy that fits our situation so well. A man slowly sinks in quicksand. On the shore sits a person offering "support." This person agrees that the problem is great and something must be done. He sympathizes and commiserates. Still the man continues sinking. All the while, a sturdy, long rope lies next to the person sitting on the shore. Yet this tangible and needed assistance is ignored. The man in the quicksand sinks to his death, never getting the help that was available, because his "counselor" offered only a listening ear.[1] Talk to someone who will offer support you can grab hold of to pull yourself out of your predicament.

4. *Select counseling or support which offers advice based on truth.* Your counselor should believe that life begins at

1. Adapted from *Counselor Training Manual* (Open ARMs, Indianapolis, 1989), pp. 1–5.

conception and that God has created that life in His own image. You won't find help if you and your counselor are at odds regarding the fact that abortion kills an unborn baby.

5. *Expect kindness from the person or people with whom you talk.* Job's "friends" leap to mind as I write this. Here was a man whose "friends" reacted improperly to his dilemma. Instead of showing compassion, they ground dirt even further into his wounds. Job needed encouragement and constructive advice, just as you do. Yet his friends called him a liar and refused to believe what he told them about his situation and his feelings. Heed Job's words when evaluating those you talk with: "For the despairing man there should be kindness from his friend; Lest he forsake the fear of the Almighty" (Job 6:14).

What are my options?

Look first to your parents, your husband, your boyfriend, or someone else close to you. A person who knows you well may be in a position to help you talk through your abortion experience. Mary Ann writes, "My husband, to whom I had told about my affair and abortion shortly after we were married, was my lifeline. He listened as I talked and cried about it over and over and he offered comfort and love. Little by little I was able to come to terms with it."

Priests and ministers are trained to counsel those in distress. If you do not belong to a church or parish, ask a trusted friend to recommend a pastor to you. As with any person, some will understand and some will reject you for your abortion. Some may reject you as a "sinner" without thinking of you as a *person* who has done something wrong. Find another counselor. However, most are understanding and can separate your act from you.

Consider talking with a lay counselor. Many crisis pregnancy centers and, of course, post-abortion groups have laypeople who are trained to gently guide aborted women through the healing process. As an added encouragement to break your silence, the counselors in these groups are often aborted women themselves.[2]

Professional counselors are an obvious outlet for your need to talk. If you choose to pursue this option, select a counseling service which views abortion as wrong and will not belittle your experience. Any counselor, lay or professional, should help you to understand and accept your responsibility for your part in your abortion. The focus should be on *you* and what you have done rather than on others and what they have done.

Another avenue for your need to talk is a support group. In our day and age there is a support group for almost every imaginable situation—alcoholics, drug users, runaways, singles, divorcées, on and on they go ad infinitum. Support groups are just what the name implies. These are groups that exist to encourage you by sharing common concerns. Abortion support groups meet regularly, usually weekly or monthly, for their members to discuss problems, share methods of coping, encourage one another by testimonies of healing, and challenge you to keep working on solving your abortion conflicts.

You may feel reluctant to join a support group. After all, you want to keep your abortion as secret as possible. Some support groups use only first names to assure confidentiality. Remember, the women present have experienced abortion. They have walked in your shoes. They share your secret as their own. You may attend only once or you may decide to come on a regular basis. Usually women are encouraged to come and go as they desire. You may meet a woman to whom you feel especially close. The two of you may form a lasting friendship as you nurture and help each other. Support groups generally meet in auditoriums of libraries, lodges, and other neutral settings which provide a nonthreatening atmo-

2. See Appendix A for listing of post-abortion support groups.

sphere—a place you will not feel uncomfortable walking into.

Bible studies help a woman to work through her abortion experience taking into account what God has to say on the subject.[3] A Bible study should be closed. That is, after the first week or two, no more women should be allowed to join until a new study begins. This serves several very important purposes. One, it limits the size to a workable number of people—usually five to ten. Two, intimacy is encouraged by having a closed group. You meet with the same women weekly for several weeks. This leads to a bond of trust which enables you to "open up" as you may not have felt able to in a less intimate group. Three, Bible studies are usually held in someone's home, which fosters a sense of comfort and relaxation.

What if I just can't reach out to someone?

If you are in despair because you believe you simply cannot go to anyone, cannot place your trust in any person regarding your experience, there is one other avenue open to you. You can talk to God. It's a natural reaction to turn to God in times of affliction, because we instinctively know we will find comfort and answers. God always listens and can give help no one else has the power to give.

"Praying" is the term used for talking to God. Luke 18:1 tells us we should pray at all times and not lose heart. Among other things, prayer rescues us from trouble (Psalms 50:15); restores righteousness (Job 33:26); and provides answers (Mark 11:24). God hears you while you are still speaking and answers as you call on Him (Isaiah 58:9). Isn't that great news!

3. Several studies have been written specifically for aborted women and are listed in Appendix C. It is recommended you work through a Bible study with a woman who will share your burden with understanding and compassion. If she, too, has had an abortion, she should be healed.

44

Remember that although talking it out with someone helps, people are fallible. Be sure you put your faith and trust in God, not in people. Other people may provide answers, but God is the originator of the answers you seek.

CHAPTER SIX

Does God Still Love Me?

"The saddest part is that it took more than ten years to realize that all I was doing was running from the one who really loved me."

Linda

When you've had an abortion, you want—you need—to know if God still loves you. It's just as when we were children and broke our mother's most valued possession by our childish carelessness (or perhaps by our disobedient romping through the house). We needed to feel her arms around us as a tangible declaration that she still loved us in spite of what we had done. That's what we are seeking when we ask, "Does God still love me?" You've "broken" something precious to God. It can't be mended. It can't be replaced. What will God's reaction be? Will He love us in spite of our disobedient action?

How does God feel about abortion?

An abortion turns our thoughts toward God and His feelings on this issue. Why? Because we have realized that abortion kills an innocent human life, a life God had some part in beginning. We wonder how He will view our part in ending that life. It's good to think about God's reaction to abortion. God has much to say about life in the womb. God gives life:

Behold, children are a gift of the Lord; The fruit of the womb is a reward. (Psalms 127:3)

And God created man in His own image, in the image of God He created him; male and female He created them. (Genesis 1:27)

Thou alone art the Lord. Thou hast made the heavens, The heaven of heavens with all their host, The earth and all that is on it, The seas and all that is in them. Thou dost give life to all of them And the heavenly host bows down before Thee. (Nehemiah 9:6)

Who among all these does not know That the hand of the Lord has done this, In whose hand is the life of every living thing, And the breath of all mankind? (Job 12:9–10)

The Spirit of God has made me, And the breath of the Almighty gives me life. (Job 33:4)

Know that the Lord Himself is God; It is He who has made us and not we ourselves. (Psalms 100:3a)

Thy hands fashioned and made me altogether. (Job 10:8a)

The God who made the world and all things in it, since He is Lord of heaven and earth, does not dwell in temples made with hands; neither is He served by human hands, as though He needed anything, since He Himself gives to all life and breath and all things. (Acts 17:24–25)

God determines the length of our lives:

The Lord kills and makes alive. (1 Samuel 2:6a)

Since his [man's] days are determined, The number of his months is with Thee, And his limits Thou hast set so that he cannot pass. (Job 14:5)

Thine eyes have seen my unformed substance; And in Thy book they were all written, The days that were ordained for me, When as yet there was not one of them. (Psalms 139:16)

God hates abortion because it terminates a life He created. We cut short God's plan for that life by taking it upon ourselves to determine when it should end.

Does God still love me?

One woman asked, "Does God sympathize with the terror one feels when faced with an unwanted pregnancy?" Laura gives us a beautiful answer: "Yes, I believe that the Lord looked at my heart. He understood my pain when I desperately needed to feel loved—although I made the wrong choice by being intimate with a boyfriend. I believe He could understand why it happened. I think He can see the denial, the lack of knowledge, etc.; but I believe that even if someone understood it all, He still forgives them freely when they repent."

As mentioned earlier, nothing surprises God. He knew before the world began that you would have an abortion.

Does that surprise *you?* It's true. Job 34:21 tells us, "For His [God's] eyes are upon the ways of a man, And He sees all his steps." That is not to say that God approves of what you did, or that He would not rather have seen you choose life—or choose to avoid conceiving that life in the first place. God hates abortion. Proverbs 6:16–19 states six things that God finds abominable, one of which is "hands that shed innocent blood." God always hates sin. But God loves *you.* Remember that God created you and gave you life. He loves you very much.

Be encouraged by these verses from the Bible regarding God's love for you:

But I [God] will not break off My lovingkindness from him, Nor deal falsely in My faithfulness. (Psalms 89:33)

Who redeemeth thy life from destruction; who crowneth thee with lovingkindness and tender mercies. (Psalms 103:4 KJV)

I [God] have loved you with an everlasting love; Therefore I have drawn you with lovingkindness. (Jeremiah 31:3)

And my soul has been rejected from peace; I have forgotten happiness. So I say, "My strength has perished, And so has my hope from the Lord." Remember my affliction and my wandering, the wormwood and bitterness. Surely my soul remembers And is bowed down within me. This I recall to my mind, Therefore I have hope. The Lord's lovingkindnesses indeed never cease, For His compassions never fail. They are new every morning; Great is Thy faithfulness. (Lamentations 3:17–23)

For I am convinced that neither death, nor life, nor angels, nor principalities, nor things present, nor things to come, nor powers, nor height, nor depth, nor any other created thing, shall be able to separate us from the love of God, which is in Christ Jesus our Lord. (Romans 8:38–39)

Does God still love you? Yes!

How does God show He still loves me?

It boggles the mind, doesn't it, to think that after the wrong we have done, God still loves us. Aren't you glad He does? Our finite, mortal minds cannot begin to comprehend the love of God toward us.

One way God shows His love for us is recorded in Romans 5:8: "But God demonstrates His own love toward us, in that while we were yet sinners, Christ died for us." God sent Christ to die in our place long before we knew we needed Him. God did this because He loves us and wanted to express that love. In fact, no one can show greater love than to die for a fellow man (John 15:13; Romans 5:7).

Did you know God searches for *us* (Luke 19:10)? That's another way He shows His love for us. Luke 15:4–7 pictures God's searching love toward us by depicting a shepherd's love for his sheep. The shepherd's love is so great for each individual sheep that when one is lost from his flock of a hundred, he leaves the ninety-nine others to search for the lost sheep. He searches until he finds it. Then the shepherd lovingly and joyfully carries it back to the fold. The passage ends, "I tell you that in the same way, there will be more joy in heaven over one sinner who repents, than over ninety-nine righteous persons who need no repentance." What a tremendous picture of God's love and concern for us!

Let's think for a moment about why God searches for us. First, we must be lost. Second, we must be of great value to Him. Third, He must want to restore us to a proper relationship with Himself (return us to the fold).

The Bible tells us we are lost and in need of a shepherd. Jesus calls Himself the Good Shepherd (John 10:11). He declares He has come to seek and to save that which is lost (Luke 19:10).

Why are we lost?

You are lost, just as every person on this earth is lost, because of sin. "Sin" is the word used to designate the things we do that God tells us *not* to do, as well as the things we don't do that God tells us *to* do. In short, sin is doing something wrong. Romans 3:23 says, "For *all* have sinned and fall short of the glory of God." Do you agree with that? Do you agree you sinned when you had an abortion? God says you did (Exodus 20:13; 23:7; Matthew 19:18; Romans 13:9a). You see, abortion is not wrong because of how our experience affects us. Abortion is wrong because God says it is wrong. Each of us has sinned. Sin is the reason we are lost.

We've already talked of the great value God places on you. He created you. He loves you. He wants to restore you to a proper relationship with Himself. This means God wants to forgive you for the wrongs—the sins—that you have done. Why? Because He loves you. God's love for you and His desire to forgive you are so intricately interwoven that they can never be separated.

CHAPTER SEVEN
Will God Forgive Me?

"God is giving me peace about it all. He has comforted me and forgiven me."

Anonymous

You may have been deeply religious prior to your abortion. You may have believed in God but not given Him much thought. Or God may have had no part in your life at all.

Now, as you begin to comprehend that you have destroyed one of God's creations, you ask yourself, "Will God forgive me?" It's a deep and sobering question. And if He would forgive, do you have the right, the courage, to approach the creator of the world to seek forgiveness for the act of murder?

Why do I need God's forgiveness?

This is a good question. We've seen that God loves us and wants to forgive us, but why do we *need* His forgiveness? On one hand, God is merciful and does not want to punish us for our sins (Numbers 14:18a). On the other hand, God is just, and so He *must* punish sin (Numbers 14:18b). Punishment for our sins results in death, spiritual death. This means that for all eternity we will be separated from the God who created and loves us. The place of separation is called hell. It is a place of torment and great sorrow (Luke 16:23–26). However, God has provided a way for us to avoid eternal punishment in hell. He provides a way for us to spend forever with Him in heaven. In heaven there will be no more tears or sorrow (Revelation 21:4). Because God is just and cannot tolerate sin, you must be forgiven in order to be reconciled to God.

What does God require for Him to forgive me?

You are going to be relieved and possibly surprised to learn that there is *nothing* you can *do* to earn God's forgiveness. Ephesians 2:8–9 tells us, "For by grace you have been saved through faith; and that not of yourselves: it is the gift of God: not as a result of works that no one should boast."

Eternal life with God is a free gift: "For the wages of sin is death, but the free gift of God is eternal life in Christ Jesus our Lord" (Romans 6:23). Isn't that wonderful! I would hate to try to earn my way to the God who created this universe. There would never be enough I could do. God knew that too. That is why He provided a way for us who are lost to be saved.

God's solution to the hopeless mess we have made of our lives is Jesus Christ. The Bible tells us Jesus Christ is God

(John 1:1) and the creator of all things (Colossians 1:16). Because of God's great love for us, He humbled Himself and took the form of a man (Philippians 2:6–8). Conceived by the Holy Spirit of God (Matthew 1:20), Jesus was born of a virgin (Matthew 1:23; Isaiah 7:14) and lived a sinless and holy life on this earth. The Bible also tells us Jesus was tempted as we are with sin, but He never sinned (Hebrews 4:15). Jesus Christ's perfection bridges the gap between us and a holy God.

Many see Jesus' living on this earth as an example of goodness and perfection for us to strive toward. Jesus came to do *more* than give us an example. He came for one primary purpose—to die in our place. Hebrews 9:22b tells us, "Without shedding of blood there is no forgiveness." Jesus did die, nearly two thousand years ago. His death was the most painful and cruel death possible—death on a cross (Philippians 2:8). He could have refused to die, but Jesus was obedient to God's will for Him. God sent Jesus to die for you and for me because He loves us. "Greater love has no one than this, that one lay down his life for his friends" (John 15:13). No tomb could hold the mighty Christ, and three days later God raised Him from the dead (1 Corinthians 15:3–4). Following His resurrection, Christ returned to heaven, where He lives once more with God the Father (Hebrews 1:3).

Do you believe God sent Jesus Christ to die for *your* sins? Believing is more than simply acknowledging in your mind that Jesus died for sinners. The Bible tells us the demons believe and tremble (James 2:19). The demons tremble because they are lost and will one day spend eternity in hell. Believing in heaven and hell and that Jesus died and was resurrected to atone for the sins of the world is not enough.

Our heart must act upon what our head believes. We call this faith—faith that God is able to and will do what He promises (Hebrews 11:6). Our faith must first include repentance (Acts 3:19). Repentance is understanding you did something wrong and deciding by an act of your will to turn away from that wrong. In order for you to repent of your sin of abortion, you must first acknowledge your part in the killing of your unborn baby. Take the responsibility for your own actions. Tell God you were wrong. That is called confession. Ask God to forgive you. I like the way Bill and Sue Banks state it: ". . . A PERSON MUST BE WILLING TO ADMIT THE SINFULNESS OF AN ACTION, IN ORDER TO BE ABLE TO CONFESS IT AND BE FORGIVEN FOR IT BY JESUS."[1] Tell God you are trusting in Christ's finished work on the cross as the *only* avenue by which God can and will forgive you (1 Timothy 2:5). Trust Christ as your personal Savior and commit your life to Him (1 John 5:11, 12). The Bible tells us in John 1:12, "But as many as received Him, to them He gave the right to become children of God. . . ." Thank God for forgiving your sin and making you His child.

Will God forgive me?

You have seen that God wants to, and will, forgive you. The only thing you must do is ask. "If we say that we have no sin, we are deceiving ourselves, and the truth is not in us. If we confess our sins, He is faithful and righteous to forgive us our sins and to cleanse us from all unrighteousness" (1 John 1:8–9). God will forgive you this very minute if you ask. You can do it by praying a simple prayer like this: "Dear Heavenly Father, I am a sinner, and I know I can do nothing to earn my way into heaven. I am sorry for my sins, including my sin of abortion. By faith alone I accept Christ's death and resurrection as payment in full for *all* my sins, and I ask Him to come and begin a new life in me. Thank you for sending Christ to pay a debt I could never repay, so I can one day spend eternity in heaven with you. Amen."

Cheryl writes, "Several months after the abortion I was hit

1. Bill and Sue Banks, *Ministering to Abortion's Aftermath* (Impact Books, Inc., Kirkwood, Missouri, 1982), p. 24.

with the reality of what I had done, and begged God's forgiveness for murdering my child and hurting the Father so much. I have never before or since felt such a deep sense of God's love and forgiveness as I did at the time of my confession. To realize that Jesus Christ died for my guilt in killing my child, took that guilt from me and laid it on Himself, never ceases to fill me with gratitude.''

Yes, but will God forgive ME?

You say, ''That's great, but will God forgive *me?''* Let me ask you a question. If God is willing and able to forgive *every* person's sins through Christ, why would you be the only exception? Why would God forgive *all* who seek forgiveness except for you? And why would He refuse to forgive you for all sins *except* your sin of abortion? If you think your sin of abortion is greater than God's power to forgive, then you have too high an opinion of yourself. God is greater than you and your sins. If the shed blood of Christ didn't cover your abortion, it wouldn't cover anything else either. It's an all-or-nothing forgiveness God offers you (Romans 4:8; Hebrews 8:12). Consider Vicky Wilde's words: ''Thank God that even though I had almost forgotten Him, He had not forgotten me, but gently and lovingly brought me to a place where I could reach out to Him and call on Him for mercy.'' She cried out to God. Won't you cry out to Christ as *your* Savior?

The *only* way to obtain God's forgiveness is through Jesus Christ, who said in John 14:6, ''I am the way, the truth, and the life; no one comes to the Father, but through Me.'' If you don't think Jesus is the answer to your problem, I challenge you to try any other method. You will find (indeed, you may already have found) that the help you get is temporary at best.

If you have placed your faith in Christ to forgive your sins, all your sins, then from this moment on your salvation is secure and your sins are forgiven. The following passage from Psalms 103:2–4; 10–13 should fill your heart with joy:

> Bless the Lord, O my soul, And forget none of His benefits; Who pardons *all* your iniquities; Who heals all your diseases; Who redeems your life from the pit; Who crowns you with lovingkindness and compassion. . . . He has not dealt with us according to our sins, Nor rewarded us according to our iniquities. For as high as the heavens are above the earth, So great is His lovingkindness toward those who fear Him. As far as the east is from the west, So far has He removed our transgressions from us. Just as a father has compassion on his children, So the Lord has compassion on those who fear Him.

Does God still love you? He tells you, "YES!" Will God forgive you? If you have placed your faith in Christ, He already has!

Although God has forgiven you, He doesn't usually just "zap" your problems away. There's still confusion and hurt to work through before you are finally healed. You've taken some BIG steps by admitting you were wrong when you aborted your baby, and by accepting the fact that you can't solve your problems without God's help. Now you can begin to sort out and resolve the other problems with which you struggle.

CHAPTER EIGHT

How Do I Cope with This Feeling of Emptiness?

"I felt empty . . . totally removed from the things around me. Others carried on and I was different."

Liz

The death of your baby has left a void. Emotional numbing following an abortion is a normal defense mechanism against the onslaught of mental pain. I believe it may occur before a woman recognizes her abortion as wrong as well as after the truth sets in. It can be akin to that initial relief. You may have felt so drained from the decision and surgery that you simply felt void of all feeling: not at peace, but not in turmoil—just drained of all emotion. As realization set in, shock may have produced an emotional withdrawal to protect you from the pain.

As with the other negative emotions which beset you

following an abortion, this feeling of emptiness is normal—to be expected, understood, and dealt with.

Why am I so numb to things in life which should bring joy (i.e. marriage, children, success in finances)?

If you have not completely dealt with your abortion, various aspects of it may still trouble your mind. You may feel you do not deserve the joy and peace which your present life brings. A bad experience in your past, even though caused by yourself, does not necessarily negate subsequent good experiences or prohibit them from occurring. However, we never find true happiness in life unless we first realize that all good gifts come from God. He gives them to us because He loves us.

If God has blessed you with a husband and children, thank Him and ask Him to show you ways to love them. If God has provided material comforts, thank Him for these also and seek to use them in ways glorifying to God. You will find that a proper response usually precedes appropriate feelings.

Is life really worth living? I contemplated suicide for several months.

Your life is the most precious thing you possess. It was given to you by God, just as your aborted baby's life was given to him by God. Do you think that killing yourself would in any way compensate the death of your baby? No. Killing yourself would only be *another* sin against the God who loves and has forgiven you. It is God who determines the length of our lives. It doesn't matter that you don't see your life as worth living. Your responsibility is to live it until God decides to take you home.

Although you may think dying now will be better than the life that lies ahead, the truth is, you don't know the wonderful things God has in store for you in this life (1 Corinthians 2:9). Look for the good. Focus on the positive. I recently counseled a woman who declared that God had never done anything good for her. Yet this woman was on a *paid leave of absence* from her job for an *entire year* in order to work through her problems; she had a close *Christian friend* (who had also had an abortion and was now healed); and she had a *pastor* who sincerely desired to help her to resolve her emotional conflicts. This woman had spent so much time focusing on her negative feelings regarding her abortion that she failed to see all the good God was bringing into her life.

Look around you, my friend—God has created a beautiful world filled with color and light and shapes and wonder. Go to a zoo or park. Sit and contemplate the beauty of life. Life. The most precious gift of all. View life through God's eyes and you will see that it *is* worth living. The worth of life is not based on your income, your physical attributes, your problems, or others' views of you. It is based on the fact that you are created in the image of God.

Yes, you killed your own child, but you are not the only person on this earth to have committed a heinous sin. If things were as they should be, a "life for a life" would be just punishment for our crime. But God in His grace has decreed you forgiven through Christ. Christ bore your punishment. Christ died that you might have life and have it more abundantly (John 10:10).

Trusting God to "save" you includes so much more than avoiding hell. God provides a means for us to live our earthly lives in joy and peace. I know how much you want that. The Bible provides answers to problems which may have plagued you for years. God wants you to live your life to its fullest. God provides the answers, but He wants you to search His Word to find and act upon them.

Why do I no longer cry at things that used to make me cry?

I think this is part of the general numbing you are feeling. Your emotions have been anesthetized for a time. Since you see your abortion as the saddest event possible, nothing else will move you to tears. It will pass.

Why do I yearn so much for the baby?

This, too, is normal. Your natural mothering instinct has been abruptly cut off. Unfulfilled. Your baby was not only a separate living individual but also flesh of your flesh. You miss him as you would miss any living child that died or was removed from you. You yearn for the completion of something begun.

Imagine you are listening to a magnificent musical composition. But wait! The orchestra suddenly ceases playing just before the final chord is resolved. You feel the need to hum or hear the end. Your abortion is like that orchestra which ceased playing. It cut short the anticipated ending and you yearn for the completion.

Is it normal to want to have another baby to make up for the other one?

Yes, but a word of caution must be given here. Many women have "replacement" pregnancies within a short time following their abortions (or miscarriages). They believe the new baby will make up for all the hurt and emptiness. Remember, each baby is a unique individual. He can never "replace" a previous child, nor should you expect him to do so.

Realize your need to grieve for that other child. Then

accept that child as dead and irreplaceable. Accept the fact that you will always be the mother of a dead baby.

Should I have another baby?

Yes. But at whatever point in time you become pregnant, remember that this new child is just that—a *new* child. Your job will be to love and nurture him without comparison to the child you aborted.

Is it truly wrong to fulfill this mothering instinct (which has nowhere else to go) with a dog? Sounds dumb, huh?

This question was submitted by a single woman with a sense of humor and a very real need. There is nothing wrong with having a pet to love. Although dogs and cats and other animals can provide companionship and pleasure, they can never replace your need for human companionship.

If you look around, you will find plenty of outlets for your mothering instinct. Instead of "mothering" a pet, consider focusing on human babies that need love. Have you ever thought of volunteering to "mother" boarder babies? Hospitals welcome people who desire to give these "unwanted" children the love and affection each human needs. You could also extend your love to shut-ins or to people in nursing homes. Establishing a close personal relationship with a human being is a challenging goal to work toward. Take time to develop a relationship with another person.

And by all means, adopt a pet and love it—just keep things in perspective.

How do I fill the void?

You can fill the void by keeping busy. Charitable organizations, work, school, parenting, reading, sewing, gardening, exercise, and a myriad of other things cry out for our attention. There is nothing wrong with this, but sometimes we *do* things in order to keep so busy we don't have time to deal with the problems in our lives. Busyness should never serve as an excuse to avoid dealing with a problem. I have a better suggestion to fill the very real void you are feeling.

When Christ left this earth to return to heaven, He did not leave us empty. He left another comforter—the Holy Spirit (1 John 3:24). If you trusted Christ as your Savior, the Holy Spirit came to dwell inside you at that moment. He will never leave you. He exists to guide, encourage, and comfort you. Ask Him to fill you with purpose. You will find new meaning in life as you seek to serve others, not out of desperation to fill the void in your own life, but out of concern to meet *their* needs.

Behind the pulpit in my church hangs a wooden cross. I've always been struck by the fact that the cross is empty. Empty. Christ no longer hangs on a cross, but is alive. When God raised Christ from the dead, He was proclaiming, "I have accepted Christ's death as sufficient to pay the price for your sins."

The beauty of the old rugged cross is that it has served its purpose. Now the cross stands empty, boldly declaring to all who will listen and believe, "The price has been paid, through Christ you are free." Because the cross is empty, I am full—full of hope and joy and peace.

CHAPTER NINE

Why Is Sex Difficult Now?

"[My abortion] affected our sexual relationship. At times I couldn't bear my husband near me. I often cried out of sheer frustration as I wondered what was happening to me."

Christine

Sexual problems can result from many underlying causes. In this chapter, sexual problems directly related to your abortion are addressed.

Why do I have such a disinterest in sex?

Following an abortion, negative thoughts can plague your mind and cause a lack of interest in continuing a sexual relationship. As Liz relates, this disinterest in sex may not surface immediately: "Three and one half years after the abortion, everything fell apart. I was so empty and unable to reach out.

I pulled away from my husband. We struggled to maintain any sexual contact at all. And I finally couldn't stand it at any time. I felt violated and forced into sex with him. We went six months without having sexual intercourse and also not touching or hugging. We were in terrible shape."

Are you afraid of something? Do you fear another pregnancy? Do you fear that becoming pregnant will lead to another abortion being forced upon you? Do you fear barrenness? Do you fear future retribution from God? Have you kept a previous affair and abortion secret from your husband? Are you afraid that during sex he will somehow find out? Do you feel betrayed by the baby's father? Do you experience physical pain during sexual intercourse? Or do you suffer with recurrent vaginal infections?[1] Any one or a combination of these could cause a disinterest in sex.

Is frigidity my punishment for having an abortion?

Frigidity means failure to become sexually aroused. This can result from various causes, some of which were just mentioned.

Examine your situation. Are you having sex with only one man—your husband? If so, are you still experiencing sexual problems? Could it be because of a physical problem? If not physical, what are your thoughts during sex? The man with whom you previously made love may have used you or been callous or forceful. You may feel guilty because of a past sexual relationship. Do you focus on these rather than on your husband?

My husband, Leigh, comments regarding our early relationship, "Concerning sex, there was always the fear of pregnancy because further children were NOT wanted—I don't know if I really knew what the reason for this was. However,

1. If you experience physical pain during sexual relations, please see your doctor as soon as possible.

many different methods of birth control were used, with great fear of their failure, and thus sex was difficult and strained. Fulfillment in sex was sought after by both, but usually wound up in frustration because of timing of birth control method or whatever."

Previous emotional trauma will affect future relationships if you allow it to control your thoughts. The negative thoughts you dwell on will eventually become part of your personality and will manifest themselves in your actions. That is why we are admonished to allow the Holy Spirit to control our thinking and actions (Ephesians 5:18). God does not punish women by making them frigid. It may be you are punishing *yourself* because of guilt you feel about your abortion. It is important to realize that usually the problems you face in this context are between you and God rather than between you and your husband.

Our relationship quickly deteriorated following my abortion. Why?

"Researcher Emily Milling found that of more than 400 couples who went through the abortion experience, most of the relationships (70%) had failed within one month after the abortion."[2]

A quote from *Aborted Women—Silent No More* answers this question:

Abortion, it seems, always underscores the weaknesses in a relationship. As an act of conditional love which reflects an unwillingness to accept an inconvenient child, abortion also implies that the relationship is viable only as long as each partner is *convenient* to the other, only as long as their separate aspirations and careers are compat-

2. As reported by Dr. Vincent M. Rue, "The Forgotten Fathers: Men and Abortion," *Heartbeat,* Fall 1984, p. 19.

ible. Thus the question "should we have a child?" slips quickly into "should we continue this relationship?" Choosing to keep the child reaffirms the relationship; choosing to abort calls the relationship into question. Especially when it is the first child of a couple's union which is being aborted, the abortion symbolically represents an unwillingness to make a deeper commitment to each other. By denying the union of their flesh, the couple denies any long-range commitment to each other.[3]

Why do I resent my husband for this? It was when we were dating that the abortion occurred.

Reasons for resentment could be that you feel your husband used you, betrayed your trust by consenting to or encouraging your abortion, or didn't really love you, but married you out of guilt because you did as he wanted and aborted your baby. Resentment is a form of anger. Dr. Jay Adams states, "Letting the sun go down on your anger is the most frequent cause of sexual disharmony in marriage. It is hard to bring all of the baggage of resentment into the bed at night and expect to have freedom of joyous sexual expression under those circumstances."[4]

Have you considered the following? "The woman gets pregnant; his first thought is to 'fix it.' If he has any feelings about the baby, the woman, or the whole situation, he is trained to deny them, and get on with the job of 'fixing it.' "[5] Here we see that the man may have consented to or advised abortion because he thought it would mend a difficult situation. He may not have realized you did not want to abort and

3. David C. Reardon, *Aborted Women—Silent No More,* (Good News Publishers, Crossway Books, Westchester, Illinois, 1988), p. 124.
4. Dr. Jay E. Adams, *The Christian Counselor's Manual* (Baker Book House, Grand Rapids, 1973), p. 359.
5. Carter Jefferson, "Men and Abortion," *National Right to Life News,* January 15, 1987, p. 20.

was trying to be supportive of your decision by saying, "Whatever you decide is okay."

We need to help our husbands, not alienate them. Sometimes they suffer as much as we do, but are unable or unwilling to express themselves. The solution to resentment is forgiveness. Only when we forgive can we enjoy and be enjoyed by our husband as God intended.

Why do I not trust even the most trustworthy gentleman in any way? (I am single.)

I believe it is a common response to think that every man will treat you as the men concerned with your abortion did. Your lack of trust may stem from unresolved bitterness toward specific men in your life. Your father may have told you to "get an abortion or get out." Your boyfriend may have betrayed your trust by refusing to marry you when you became pregnant. Doctors are usually men, and you may blame your doctor for his part in performing your abortion. Betrayal is a mighty force in inhibiting one's willingness to trust. In order to free yourself so you are willing to open the door you have shut, you need to forgive each man involved in your abortion. Evaluate each man you meet individually rather than stereotyping him into the mold you have cast.

Are my sexual problems directly related to my abortion or to the promiscuity that followed my abortion?

In most of our situations, abortion is tangible evidence of involvement in sexual immorality. You may have sought the abortion to keep secret your sin. Others may not know, but you know. You may unconsciously transfer your guilt to your current relationship. Also, because the abortion has not been dealt with, emotional attachment to the baby's father remains and may intrude on your new relationship.

For instance, you may have determined that you are "dirty" because of your abortion or previous promiscuity. One woman explains, "I know I'm healed and forgiven, but there is one area that I haven't gotten a grip on. That is my sexual relation with my husband. I don't feel worthy, I still feel cheap and dirty and don't enjoy my husband like I should."

Another woman comments similarly: "My main problem is regarding my sexual relation with my husband. I don't enjoy it. I still feel dirty and not worthy to have the kind of relation that God would want us to have."

Still another woman states the problem this way: "Sometimes my attitude is don't touch me, other times my attitude is fine. I believe it is old guilt from a sinful relationship with ex-boyfriend and possibly past abortion."

If you were promiscuous following your abortion, your current sexual problems may stem from unresolved guilt over your promiscuity compounded by the guilt of your abortion. Your promiscuity may have been a way of physically validating your feelings of worthlessness. Indiscriminate sex may have been used to escape facing up to your abortion. The only way to eliminate the problem is to face your guilt and deal with it.

Is sex ever wrong?

Sexual intercourse is a beautiful, sensual, and fulfilling act created by God to meet a partner's need within the marriage relationship. The Bible tells us it is wrong to *abstain* from sex within the context of marriage unless it is for a period of fasting and prayer. That same passage explains that our bodies are not ours but our marriage partner's (see 1 Corinthians 7:1–5). That is why pursuit of sexual pleasure as an end in itself leads to despair. We are to pursue sex to meet our partner's need by fully giving what already is theirs—ourselves.[6]

What about continuing to have sex after the abortion if you're not married?

A college girl called me recently with the complaint that sex with her boyfriend had been difficult since her abortion. She related sex was no longer fun. She felt dirty and guilty about the entire situation. She wanted to know what she could do to correct the problem.

This young woman's problem went further than mixed feelings over her abortion. Now she felt guilt whenever she had sex with her boyfriend because her conscience told her she was doing something wrong. Sex had become unclean to her, not because she *thought* it was unclean, but because her abortion had helped her realize that sex outside of marriage is wrong.

As we finished our conversation, the young woman said, "Thanks. I knew what I had to do, but I needed to hear it from someone else."

God reserves sex for marriage for two reasons. One is that the sexual union is symbolic of Christ and His bride, the Church. It represents completeness and perfection. The other is that sex is the vehicle by which human beings reproduce. In other words, having sex can result in a new person coming into existence. God has established marriage and the family unit. God in His wisdom planned for children to be born after marriage and into a loving family environment. It doesn't always happen that way, but that is the way it was meant to be.

Women often abstain from sex for a short time following their abortion. Then rational thinking takes over, and the

6. The Song of Solomon offers insights into the joy of a married love relationship. See also Proverbs 5:18–19.

thought "It could never happen again" leads us to reestablish the old relationship with our boyfriend, or to start a new one with a different man.[7]

What steps can I take to enjoy lovemaking with my husband?

Often, as I did, in our quest to resolve our abortions, we overlook the obvious act of seeking forgiveness for things that led to our abortions. Have you ever asked God to forgive you for the sin of having a sexual relationship with a man prior to marriage? If not, do that first.

Second, have you gone to your husband and asked his forgiveness for having sex prior to your marriage? A pastor once pointed out in a sermon that having sex with a person other than one's own husband or wife, even if you eventually marry that person, is a sin against the spouse. It was a tremendous healing for me when I asked Leigh to forgive me for not coming to him a virgin. It strengthened our relationship, and we were able to start clean before God in our sexual relationship.

Once you have received God's and your husband's forgiveness, do the following:

1. Explain to your husband that you are having difficulties. Ask for his patience and suggestions.
2. Gradually lead up to the sex act—kiss, hug, fondle. Sexual intercourse is not necessary each time you "cuddle."
3. Ask God to remove ugly thoughts and replace them with good ones (Romans 12:1–2).
4. Strive to please your husband during the sex act (1 Corinthians 7:4).

7. One caution I want to add in this age of AIDS is that if you are not involved in a monogamous relationship, your chances of contracting this deadly disease are greatly increased.

71

5. Don't expect an orgasm each time you have sex.
6. Be patient! It may take time for sex to become enjoyable for you without having to "work" at it.

Laura adds a final comment: "I do feel the pain of abortion affects a sexual relationship with a husband; but I believe that 'In all these things we are more than conquerors through him that loved us' (Romans 8:37). God can and is restoring my trust in an intimate relationship. It does take time and needs healing."

CHAPTER TEN

Why Do I Feel So Worthless?

"I have been through a living hell because of my lack of faith and my need to please others at the cost of losing myself. I've learned a hard lesson, but one I won't have to repeat."

Liz

As we answer the question which titles this chapter, it is important to realize that not all of the problems we face are a direct result of our abortion. In addition to creating new problems, an abortion often accentuates preexisting difficulties. Instead of blaming your abortion for all your problems, view it as a catalyst to recognizing and sorting out your feelings in order to better understand what "makes you tick" and how to make you "tick" better.

Why do I feel worthless?

Feelings of worthlessness result from various impressions you perceive. Your feelings of worthlessness may originate in your childhood. You may have been emotionally or physically abused by parents or other authority figures. You may have been unwanted by your parents or unable to meet their expectations for you. Feelings of worthlessness may have to do with external appearances—flaws you see in yourself. In my case, I was an awkward and plain child. Peers often made fun of my skinny legs and large nose. My self-esteem was lowered with each thrust of verbal spears thrown at me.

A shameful act such as your abortion may have left you with feelings of worthlessness.

> I feel the message I am to give others is that when you take an unborn life, you devalue that life, and in the process, your own inner respect for the value of *your* life is diminished. The destruction of that understanding of your own worth as one created in God's image results in the gradual or sudden breakdown of the inner strength of your life, and may result in the [eventual] destruction of it. The Scriptures are true, "Be not deceived, God is not mocked: for whatsoever a man soweth, that shall he also reap" (Galatians 6:7). (Anonymous)

Thoughts such as "I am the only one to have done such a terrible thing" or "No one could ever love or forgive me for what I have done" seem to confirm your worthlessness. Continued feelings of guilt rob life of all meaning. One demoralized woman tells it this way:

> Abortion is a way of telling a mom, the world doesn't need you or your kid, and besides, what makes you think you deserve to have children? It's like saying, this fetus

is a blob of tissue because so are you. You're just a product of the baby boom, an unnecessary human being who takes up space and makes the world more crowded and polluted. We'd get rid of all you extras, but since we don't want to be too obvious about it, we'll just make sure we don't have any more extras coming from a lot of extras.

Satan also challenges us with being worthless.[1] He puts vague yet subtle thoughts into our minds regarding our worth. God forgave all sin at the cross of Calvary. But Satan wants us to focus on the bad we did rather than on the forgiveness we have received. Since God refuses to punish us for the wrong we did, we sometimes decide to punish ourselves by focusing on our own inadequacies.

What is the difference between self-esteem and self-image?

Self-esteem can be defined as a belief in or respect for yourself. Self-image refers to your conception or idea of yourself, that is, how you look at yourself and how you think others perceive you. Both work together to establish your evaluation of your worth.

How does low self-image affect me?

Dr. David Seamands states, "The way you *look at* yourself and *feel about* yourself, way deep down in the heart of your personality—so you will be and so you will become. What

1. The devil is crafty but not wise. If you resist him, he will leave you alone (James 4:7).

75

you see and feel will determine your relationships both with other people and with God."[2]

A low self-image can keep us from seeing the reality of a situation. We may find ourselves trying to prove ourselves, always needing to be right, being self-centered, wondering about our worth, maneuvering others to reassure us of our worth.[3]

A low self-image affects our self-esteem. Sometimes *we* perceive ourselves differently than others see us. Sometimes our perceptions are incorrect. Because *we* know of flaws in our appearance or faults in our character, we believe everyone sees them and judges us by these faults. For instance, several weeks ago I didn't "feel good" about myself. I was fifteen pounds overweight, and my hair looked scraggly and yucky. In spite of my personal view of myself, people told me how good my figure is after four children, and they commented favorably on my hair. But *I* knew things weren't as perfect as they could be. When I'm having a "down" day, it matters little what others say. There were things I could do to improve my self-esteem. I had my hair cut in a new style and went on a diet. Simple! In this instance, yes. However, deep-seated feelings of worthlessness take more than altering outward appearances to correct.

What determines our worth?

Trying to measure our lives by other people's standards leads to despair. We end up being and doing what we really don't want to be or do. Although a good self-image and positive self-esteem refer to our view of, and belief in, ourselves, these attitudes should not result from what *we* or *others* think *about* us. The value we place upon ourselves should result

2. Dr. David A. Seamands, *Healing for Damaged Emotions* (Victor Books, Wheaton, Illinois, 1981), p. 60.
3. Ibid., p. 72.

from understanding our position in Christ. The Bible tells us we are *fully accepted* in the Beloved (Jesus Christ) and that we are God's own possession (Ephesians 1:6, 14).

Our worth is not based on others' opinions of us, nor on our own evaluation of ourselves. God establishes our worth. Stop judging yourself by others' standards and look at yourself by God's standards. Sounds scary, huh? But we often judge ourselves more harshly than God judges us. Christians *are* worthy to stand in God's presence without fear of personal condemnation because God sees us as perfect and righteous through Christ. "He [God] has made Him [Jesus] who knew no sin to be sin on our behalf, that we might become the righteousness of God in Him" (2 Corinthians 5:21; see also Romans 3:21–26; Philippians 3:9).

Your worth comes from the value *God* places on you. *Everything* God created is of value if only for the reason that God thought enough of it to bring it into being. In Matthew 10:29–31 Jesus says, "Are not two sparrows sold for a cent? And yet not one of them will fall to the ground apart from your Father. But the very hairs of your head are numbered. Therefore do not fear; you are of more value than many sparrows." Imagine, as insignificant as the sparrow is, not one falls to the ground without God knowing about it! But people are of far greater value than many sparrows. God created *you* in His own image (Genesis 1:26). You are so important to God that He knows the number of hairs on your head! Your physical appearance, intellect, and emotions were allowed by God to come together to form a unique person—you. Most important, you are so valuable that God sent Jesus to die for you. When you downgrade yourself, it's like slapping God in the face.

Allow God to love you! Your value is inestimable. After all, God created you! God loves you—let Him!

What is depression?

Following an abortion, we may feel down or discouraged. This is normal and to be expected; it is not depression. The problem becomes serious when we develop "I" trouble. This is the "woe is me" pity party. Dwelling on the negative aspects of an abortion and surrounding events to the exclusion of anything else leads us into depression. We focus on ourselves and our problems until we find ourselves in despair. Feelings of worthlessness and hopelessness drag us to depths from which we can never climb out on our own. It is when we are in the depths of depression that we often reach upward and outward to God, instinctively realizing only He can help us.

A classic description of depression is found in Psalms 38:1–11. Read it and see if you find yourself in King David's words:

O LORD, rebuke me not in Thy wrath; And chasten me not in Thy burning anger. For Thine arrows have sunk deep into me, And Thy hand has pressed down on me. There is no soundness in my flesh because of Thine indignation; There is no health in my bones because of my sin. For my iniquities are gone over my head; As a heavy burden they weigh too much for me. My wounds grow foul and fester. Because of my folly, I am bent over and greatly bowed down; I go mourning all day long. For my loins are filled with burning; And there is no soundness in my flesh. I am benumbed and badly crushed; I groan because of the agitation of my heart. Lord, all my desire is before Thee; And my sighing is not hidden from Thee. My heart throbs, my strength fails me; And the light of my eyes, even that has gone from me. My loved ones and my friends stand aloof from my plague; And my kinsmen stand afar off.

Reread this passage. If you have ever been deeply depressed, you understand how David felt. Notice that David's depression affected him physically, mentally, emotionally, and spiritually.

How can feelings of worthlessness manifest themselves?

In answering this question, I struggle with this: do feelings of worthlessness lead to depression, or does depression lead us into feelings of worthlessness? I believe the two are intertwined. When we feel worthless we lean toward depression because our eyes are on ourselves and our imagined lack of value. We can focus inwardly so long that depression results. However, when we are depressed, our feelings of self-worth plunge to their lowest depths. Depression results in self-condemnation. We believe we can do nothing right. We trust no one—not even ourselves. We view ourselves as failures. Outward actions and reactions unconsciously reflect what we are feeling inwardly. But beware! Our feelings may err and impair our judgment.

In an attempt to escape or justify feelings of worthlessness, we sometimes pursue activities which (although it may take us time to realize it) only serve to intensify our feelings of worthlessness. We may turn to drugs, sexual promiscuity, physical and emotional abuse of others (particularly children), alcohol, obesity, anorexia, over- or under-achieving, paranoia, or suicide as outlets for our feelings of inadequacy.

The following women tell you ways in which they tried to "prove" their worthlessness:

After the abortion a "friend" insisted that I sleep with him so that I wouldn't become frigid about sex. I slept with more men than I can count looking for a little love and affection. They were *all* so willing and soon left me more devastated than before. I was a whore but didn't even get paid for my stupidity. (Denise Lackey)

I was hospitalized for severe depression and placed under suicide watch. I had a plan to take my life. . . . People were shocked when they heard I was hospitalized for mental and emotional problems. Up till then I had them all fooled. All but God, that is! He saw the pain that drove me to the cemetery three or four days a week. It was so peaceful there! The thought of dying became more appealing as I walked between the tombstones straightening floral arrangements, searching for my baby. After all, the cemetery is a place for the dead. . . . At work I'd sit and cry. I just couldn't handle routine things anymore. . . . I planned my death. I was going to drive to my peaceful cemetery, swallow a bottle of sleeping pills and cut my wrists. I wanted to make sure I'd die. . . . (Paulette Hawkins)

They never tell you of the emotional trauma you go through after the abortion. I have attempted suicide twice, had numerous failed relationships because of my deep hate I had for all men, got involved with drugs and alcohol to help me forget. I have faked pregnancy hoping to bring him back, and now as a mother I feel as if I have to [make up] for what I did four years ago by being a [supermom]. (Anonymous)

I have in the past struggled with a subconscious desire to punish myself (because the Lord didn't) by psychosomatic illnesses—my body would have symptoms, etc. I realize this and prayed I would see myself through the Lord's eyes, that I would have compassion on myself. (Laura)

Over the years as a counselor I've noted that many girls who return to pregnancy help centers . . . often deliberately get themselves pregnant again as a means of helping them to come to terms with an earlier abortion. Often because they feel it can take the place of a baby already lost, especially where an abortion has been pressured by family and friends. They yearn for something to call their own. (Christine)

What is this reaction accomplishing?

We have read how King David's depression manifested itself. He became physically ill and weak, his unconfessed sins burdened him as a heavy weight, his troubled mind deprived David of peace, and his demeanor caused family and friends to shy away from him.

Living out feelings of worthlessness and permitting yourself to become depressed result in a wasted life and ruined relationships. You can run thousands of miles to escape a problem, but when you arrive at your destination, your problems will still be with you. You can't run away from yourself. You must face yourself and learn to live with who you are and what you have done.

How should I respond to depression?

The best antidote for depression is to take positive action. Depression increases as we neglect our responsibilities. As work piles up, depression deepens. No wonder people get depressed when they sit idly in front of a TV for hours or lie in bed bemoaning their situation! Their inactivity intensifies their depression. On the other hand, those who pursue self-debasing lifestyles, as confirmation of or escape from their inner turmoil, need to withdraw from their hopeless activity and concentrate on living responsibly.

God tells us not to dwell on evil (1 Thessalonians 5:22; Psalms 34:14, 141:4). Our act of abortion was evil. When you continue to dwell on it by refusing to relinquish thoughts of your abortion and how horribly guilty you feel, or when you refuse to deal with your problems God's way, you are committing sin against God. In order to receive permanent

81

and complete healing, you should focus on God and on doing what He requests. Philippians 4:8 provides excellent advice: "Finally, brethren, whatever is true, whatever is honorable, whatever is right, whatever is pure, whatever is lovely, whatever is of good repute, if there is any excellence and if anything worthy of praise, let your mind dwell on these things."

To have victory over feelings of worthlessness and depression, you must put your emotions under the control of God (Galatians 5:1). I know things may be bad for you right now, but you have God's promises that they are not hopeless. Remember King David's words of utter despair? He resolved his depression by confessing his sin and asking for God's help (Psalms 38:18, 22). You can do that too. Fill your mind with God-honoring thoughts—songs of praise or prayers for yourself or for others; look up God's promises and memorize them; seek counsel from others; be with other people—don't sit in a room by yourself and brood; ask God to prick your conscience when you begin to focus on your abortion.

Situations in your life occur because God allows them for your own good—to mature you, to teach you, to strengthen you. Look for God's purpose in your life. What goal is He trying to accomplish through you? Are your attitudes and actions helping or hindering that goal? Thank God for already having forgiven your past sins and claim Romans 15:13 for yourself: "Now may the God of hope fill you with all joy and peace in believing, that you may abound in hope by the power of the Holy Spirit."

Focus on God healing you. We have no inner strength, only stubborn wills. Good inner feelings do not always equal true inner healing. Focusing inwardly and rehashing your abortion time and again won't help you, because the solutions to your problems lie not within your own mind, but with God. The real need is to focus your eyes outwardly (Psalms 116:3–4).

You are going to have "off" days when you aren't at your best. Everybody has them. We are to place ourselves under the control of the Holy Spirit[4] no matter what our inner feelings. God does not excuse poor behavior because of the way we feel.

I like to give the people I counsel "homework" assignments (must be the schoolteacher in me!). Here's an assignment for you: For one week keep a daily log of reasons and situations in which you feel sorry for yourself. Then set to work correcting wrong thinking, following the format outlined in Chapter 21 (under the subheading "What are the steps to complete healing?").

Is there any hope for real change?

I know, you're probably thinking, "yes, but will I ever *really* be able to change—will I ever *feel* like I'm worth something?" Because abortion is a negative in our life, the surrounding emotions tend to be negative. Dwelling on the negatives long enough will have disastrous effects, because what we think and how we act are directly related. "For as he thinks within himself, so is he" (Proverbs 23:7).

You *feel* worthless because you or others have convinced yourself you *are* worthless because you had an abortion (or for some other reason). Because you believe you are worthless, you have been trying to persuade *others* that you *are* as worthless as you believe yourself to be. Thank God our feelings don't determine our worth! And thank God we *can* change our concept of ourselves and our feeling of self-worth to reflect God's estimation of us.

In part, you experience self-hatred and thoughts of worthlessness because of negative emotions that have built up inside of you—emotions such as guilt, grief, anger, or hate. Yet it lies within God's power to turn each of these negatives into

4. To place yourself under the control of the Holy Spirit means that by an act of your will you choose to allow God to guide and influence your thoughts and actions.

a positive. Guilt becomes pardon. Grief becomes peace. Anger extends the hand of forgiveness. Hate resolves into love. And as these emotions find positive solutions, your self-hatred will become acceptance of who and what you are. Your feelings of worthlessness will dispel as you begin to view yourself as God views you.

Dr. Jay Adams states:

> While the Scriptures everywhere acknowledge the important place of habit and faithfully describe the hard struggle to put off old sinful ways, they also ring with the assurance that by the Word and the Spirit radical changes are possible *at any point in life and regardless of what one's background may have been like.* There is hope for great change in the gospel of Jesus Christ. Therefore, when a child becomes a Christian, he must be taught that much of what he has learned to do previously must be changed. The former sinful manner of life developed by others and by himself must be replaced by godly ways of living.[5]

Hope for change lies in your willingness to believe and act upon God's Word. You are of great worth. God says so.

5. Dr. Jay E. Adams, *The Christian Counselor's Manual* (Baker Book House, Grand Rapids, 1973), p. 139.

CHAPTER ELEVEN

I Have a Right to Be Angry, Don't I?

"Angry? Of course I'm angry! My abortion took my baby's life and left me in a state of devastation."

Pam

You've been hurt and now you're angry. That's probably an understatement, isn't it? Actually, you're weighed down with bitterness or hate or rage over the lies and deception that helped convince you to abort your baby. Since anger is one of the most common emotions aborted women experience, let's take a look at what it is, what causes it, and what we can do about it.

What is anger?

"Anger" is the generic term for emotions usually expressed by ventilation (blowing up) or internalization (clamming up).[1] Blowing up is aimed at hurting others and may include impatience, indignation, sarcasm, hostility, vengefulness, ire, rage, fury, or wrath. Clamming up focuses your energy on your own self, resulting in resentment, frustration, bitterness, brooding, irritability, and depression. Any one of the various forms of anger can consume your thoughts, your actions, and ultimately your life if left unresolved.

What causes anger?

Anger is caused by physical or emotional hurts that are not resolved; injustices to ourselves or others that aren't corrected; and the inability or failure to control our circumstances. If you look at specific reasons for becoming angry regarding abortion, you will see they fit into one of the above categories:

- Getting pregnant
- Realization a human being was aborted
- Lack of information prior to the abortion decision
- Being lied to
- Betrayal of trust
- Sense of worthlessness
- Compromise of values
- Poor medical care
- Involuntary sterilization

1. Dr. Jay E. Adams, *The Christian Counselor's Manual* (Baker Book House, Grand Rapids, 1973), p. 349.

Anger can be directed at people or events. We can become angry with ourselves because of our stupidity or selfishness. We can become angry with others—doctors, father of baby, men in general, parents, friends, counselors, clinic—because of lies, encouragement, or actions. We can even become angry with people not having any connection with our abortion, such as pregnant women because they have what we now want, or with other children. And we can become angry with God for not stopping the abortion.[2]

If God has forgiven me, why am I still so angry and bitter?

Being forgiven by God doesn't mean He also wipes out our emotions and memories. It does mean we now have a way to resolve our problems—God's way. If you draw on God's power through Bible study, prayer, and applying biblical principles to your life, your anger and bitterness will eventually be replaced with love and peace.

I'm hurting inside so much. I don't want people to know. How can I keep it from showing?

Many women sacrificed their unborn baby in an attempt to salvage a relationship, only to lose their boyfriend or husband. That hurts. Many women can't have more children because of complications related to their abortion. That hurts.

2. I answered the question "Why did God allow this to happen?" in Chapter 1. In our grief, it's easy to become bitter against God. That does not give us the right to shake our fist at God over the fact that He "let" us get pregnant. Diane has a healthy attitude about her abortion: "Why did God let this happen to me? My pregnancies and abortions were consequences of sinful choices I made." Don't get mad at God. Trust Him during the hard times. Turn to God and ask Him to reveal the depths of your despair. Then apply His Word to your wounds.

Your emotions are probably topsy-turvy and you think no one understands. That hurts. The hurts you feel are deep and real.

Tragically, in order to keep their hurt from showing, many women push their hurt deep inside themselves, hoping it will never dig its way out. When it does, they are shocked, terrified at the renewed intensity of the feelings they buried and tried to forget.

It's okay to admit you hurt. And it helps to understand that we usually react negatively to situations and people when we are hurting. That makes the hurt hard to hide. Here are ten reactions that indicate a person is hurting inside:

1. Showing a lack of concern for others
2. Being overly sensitive and touchy (thinks others are always talking about her)
3. Possessiveness with friends; rarely having any close friends
4. Having a tendency to avoid meeting new people
5. Showing little or no gratitude
6. Usually speaking words of empty flattery or harsh criticism
7. Holding grudges against people, sometimes for a long time—unforgiving
8. Exhibiting a stubborn or sulky attitude
9. Unwillingness to share or help anyone
10. Being prone to extreme mood changes (either very "up" or very "down").[3]

Look at yourself. Are you happy? Are you at peace? Or are you in turmoil—churning inside? Trying to hide your hurt by keeping it buried inside of you only hurts you more. Hurting inside can be an indicator that bitterness is brewing. God tells you to beware of bitterness because it springs up and

3. Winkie Pratney, "Hurt and Bitterness" (Last Days Ministries, Lindale, Texas, 1984), pamphlet.

multiplies until it overtakes you (Hebrews 12:15). What you need to do is release yourself from the bondage of your hurt in a beneficial and nonviolent way.

What will help to repair my hurt?

Following are seven principles to help you to effectively repair your hurt:

1. Understand most hurts come from carelessness and are not inflicted on purpose (people weren't trying to hurt you when they encouraged you to abort).
2. Recognize healing of hurts is hastened when the *offender* is blessed (treat those who hurt you kindly and with love).
3. Give your hurts to God—it's okay to tell God how hurt you are.
4. Remember that hurts are usually temporary.
5. Acknowledge hurts are deepened by retaliation.
6. Don't wallow in self-pity when hurt.
7. Be assured there is healing in forgiveness.[4]

Think about these principles. Act upon them. With time your hurts can heal, but only if you *want* them to heal and work toward that goal.

What can I do to resolve my anger?

Life is going to present us with situations that anger us. Resolving each incidence of anger as it occurs should be our goal.

I have a confession to make. Right now I'm frustrated and irritable because I have four kids running around the house (acting just like kids!); I have a publisher's deadline looming

4. Adapted from *The Marriage Repair Kit* (no other information available).

only a few hours away; and I'm having difficulty putting my thoughts into words which will help you to deal with your anger.

When I need to resolve *my* anger these are the steps I take:

1. I admit I am angry;
2. I determine the source of my anger—in this case frustration over a task to be completed;
3. I admit I have *chosen* to allow a particular situation anger me;
4. I desire to be free of my anger;
5. I ask God's forgiveness for my sinful response to my anger;
6. I ask God to help me resolve the situations that led to my becoming angry; and then
7. I choose to walk away from my anger and not grab it back again. I accomplish this, with God's help, by refusing to keep mulling over in my mind the circumstances which led to my becoming angry.

Anger keys you up. For the past several hours I haven't been thinking clearly because all my energies were going into my mounting anger rather than into accomplishing the goal before me.

Writing this section has helped me to better understand my own anger and how to deal with it when it rears its ugly head again (and it will). I trust you will find help here too.

How should I react toward those involved with my abortion?

There are two common reactions to anger. One is to adopt what I call "The Incredible Hulk syndrome." Someone hurts you, and you lash out at him or her in a fury of rage. You turn from an ordinarily gentle person into a monster.[5] The other response to anger involves "controlling" your anger by keeping it chained inside of you. Neither response resolves the problem and may ultimately cause great harm to you or others.

In order to respond appropriately to those involved in your abortion, you must first cleanse your own heart. I believe you will find Psalms 51:10–13 a good model to use in asking God to cleanse you.

Before responding to those involved in your abortion, commit yourself to changing your attitude. By an act of your will, lay your sinful anger aside. However, when you put off anger, you must put on something in its place. Pity, sorrow, love, compassion, and forgiveness should be your response toward those involved in your abortion. Jesus teaches something no other prophet taught. He teaches us to love our enemies (Matthew 5:43–48). We are told to love God first, then our neighbors as ourselves (Mark 12:30–33). It's interesting that we must first love ourselves in order to love our neighbors! If you hate yourself because of your abortion, you can't love your neighbor. When you think of neighbors, remember that your "enemies" are your neighbors too.

Like anger, love is an emotion. But unlike anger, love must be learned. God would not tell you to love if He did not enable you to accomplish it. "Beloved, let us love one another, for love is from God; and everyone who loves is born of God and knows God. The one who does not love does not know God, for God is love" (1 John 4:7–8).

If we love those involved in our abortion, we will seek to direct our anger to their good. Love demands that sin be dealt with. This means we must confront those involved in our abortions. Dr. Adams states, "Turning anger towards the problem, however, almost always involves confronting

5. It's helpful to understand that although ranting and raving may *appear* to make you feel better, it serves no helpful purpose and only makes others angry and upset.

another in anger. Yet the *way* in which they are confronted makes the difference. They must be *confronted* to the extent that they are involved *responsibly* in the solution to the problem. They are confronted not in order to embarrass or hurt them, but to help them to move in the proper directions. The purpose for the confrontation is to help them to solve the problem (Ephesians 4:29)."[6]

It is impossible to love someone and not forgive him or her. Forgiveness implies heartfelt love. I know at this point you probably don't *feel* love toward those people who hurt you, nor do you want to forgive them. You will find if you, by an act of your will and in dependence on God, forgive and love those involved in your abortion, the appropriate feelings will eventually follow. Taking our eyes off ourselves and the wrongs done to us will help us to look at others and forgive. Focus your energies on finding the solution to the other person's *problem* with respect to your abortion rather than on the *person* who made the problem.

What about the people who are making money by killing unborn babies?

The same solutions apply to these people also. Sometimes it's frustrating to see others continue to do wrong. Because *we* know the truth, we expect *everyone* to know the truth and act upon it. We don't understand why God allows abortion to continue. It will help you to understand that "when the sentence for a crime is not quickly carried out, the hearts of the people are filled with schemes to do wrong. Although a wicked man commits a hundred crimes and still lives a long time, I know that it will go better with God-fearing men, who are reverent before God" (Ecclesiastes 8:11–12 NIV). Know that those involved in abortion will be punished one day by God if they do not repent (turn away from their sin). At the

6. Adams, *The Christian Counselor's Manual,* p. 354.

same time, use your anger constructively to help people avoid God's anger by guiding them away from their evil ways.

I still feel angry sometimes toward my former boyfriend who wanted me to get the abortion. How can I deal with this bitterness once and for all?

Although you may have forgiven your boyfriend (or parents or husband), feelings of resentment can crop into your thoughts. At those times you should consciously ask God's Holy Spirit to control and focus your thoughts on something else. Our object is to live in peace with ourselves and others (2 Corinthians 13:11), and that can only occur when we yield ourselves to the Holy Spirit.

I find it nearly impossible to trust medical personnel. I wonder how to decide on doctors and, sometimes, whether or not to follow through on their advice. What do you suggest?

My first suggestion is to forgive in your heart before God the medical personnel involved in your abortion. Next, actively seek physicians who do not refer patients for or perform abortions. Finally, ask yourself, "Have I stopped eating just because Mom once burned my dinner?" People make mistakes. Some mistakes are harder to live with than others. It is wrong to judge everyone by the mistakes someone else has made.

How should I feel about the guy who got me pregnant? How do I act around him? I see him every once in a while due to mutual friends.

You should feel sadness over the relationship which resulted in your becoming pregnant outside of marriage. You should hurt for the man who has lost his unborn son. Because I lived through this very situation several years ago, I know how difficult it can be to come into association with your aborted baby's father. One thing that helped me was to realize that I played an equal part in becoming pregnant. It allowed me to forgive my ex-boyfriend for his role in our relationship.

What if someone doesn't know I'm angry with them?

Oftentimes people do not realize they have said or done something which has deeply affected you. For instance, when my parents heard I was pregnant, they wanted me to have and keep the baby, their first grandchild. But as we talked, my mother said, "You know, Pam, you will have to quit school to care for the baby." That one sentence closed my mind to the reality of the baby to be born and opened my mind to the possibility of terminating the pregnancy. Although my mother was not aware of it, my anger toward her grew for years as I blamed her for her callousness at that moment in my life. She was not even aware that her words had affected me so adversely. She is a practical woman and was merely stating a fact I needed to consider. She never dreamed that leaving school was my worst fear with regard to my pregnancy. The very logistics of finishing my education and caring for a child had been foremost on my mind. My mom had no idea of the anger and resentment my mind had built up due to her words.

The fact that the other person may not know you harbor

angry thoughts toward him or her does not negate your responsibility to forgive. Because my parents did not know how angry I was, I chose to forgive them in my heart before God. Since then, I have had an opportunity to explain why I had been angry with them. They appreciated knowing what had been going on in my mind.

The other side of the coin is that you may find the person knew all along you were angry with him or her. Anger is difficult to conceal. It comes out in our words, actions, and expressions. Don't be too sure that the other person doesn't know how you feel. You might approach him or her with the statement "I don't know if you realize it or not, but I've been harboring some wrong thoughts toward you regarding my abortion." That opens the door for the other person to express his or her thoughts. Communication is vital in resolving abortion conflicts. Unfortunately, it is too often lacking.

What will happen if I don't resolve my anger?

If you refuse to resolve your anger, you may find yourself using that anger to condone your abortion or to confuse the issue. You may allow your anger to exit through your mouth in gossip or in speaking evil of those involved in your abortion. You may develop an "I'll get you" mentality and seek revenge from those who were involved in your abortion. You may swing to extremes, becoming either violent or totally withdrawn. You may even become physically ill. One thing is certain—as long as you remain angry, you will never heal.

Does God get angry about abortion?

Yes. Abortion wrenches the heart of God. Proverbs 6:16–19 tells us God finds abortion (shedding of innocent blood) abominable. He is angry with the wicked every day (Psalms 7:11).[7]

Those who continue their involvement in the pro-abortion movement will not go unpunished. "Be sure of this: The wicked will not go unpunished, but those who are righteous will go free" (Proverbs 11:21 NIV; see also Exodus 34:6–7).

Does anger ever serve a good purpose?

Yes. Anger is an emotion. Our emotions were given to us by God. Therefore, any emotion can be used for good. However, emotions in themselves are neither good nor bad. Any emotion can become constructive or destructive, depending upon how we respond to it. Anger is a tremendously powerful emotion. To attempt to turn it off or deny it is wrong. Instead, we must seek constructive methods of directing it.

Anger is not sinful when its expression is *justified* and *controlled.* For example, you *should* be angry at the fact of abortion. Anger over something evil or wrong is justified. This type of anger is often referred to as "righteous indignation" and is exemplified in Jesus' cleansing of the temple (Matthew 21:12–13). Although Jesus was angry, He dealt with the situation in a decisive but sinless manner (Hebrews 4:15).

Since God is perfect, we know God never sins in His anger. Always He directs His anger at correcting a specific problem. Being imperfect human beings, we must be careful we don't use a righteous cause as a platform to vent sinful anger. Being justified in your cause is not enough. Your anger must also be released under control. When I am responding to anger in a righteous manner, I have inner peace, and am under control outwardly. Then after prayer I earnestly

7. There are several other specific events in the Bible which incurred God's anger. For examples, see 1 Kings 11:9–10; Deuteronomy 9:7; Isaiah 5:20–25.

96

seek to correct the situation in a way that allows people to see Christ in me.

Did you know God *tells* us to be angry? However, we must be careful to respond to our anger properly. In the same verse that God tells us to be angry, He also tells us not to sin in our anger (Ephesians 4:26). Anger becomes sinful when we focus it on people and things rather than on the problem. If we are to be angry and not sin, the words of our mouths and meditations of our hearts must be pure (Psalms 19:14). Righteous anger properly directed and under control always aims for constructive and positive change.

Abortion angers me personally. I find the laws surrounding abortion to be absurd. Doctors work feverishly to save prematurely born babies, while in the same hospital doctors kill babies the same age because their moms don't want them. Yes, our laws make me angry. What do I do? I write and speak (in love) to educate people about the truth. My anger is used constructively to correct the problem.

Whenever we find ourselves in a situation that might cause us to feel or express anger in one of its various forms, we would do well to meditate on these words: "But let everyone be quick to hear, slow to speak and slow to anger; for the anger of man does not achieve the righteousness of God" (James 1:19b–20).

CHAPTER TWELVE
Must I Forgive Others?

"I didn't know it would take so long to get over it or that I would have to forgive so many people."

Christine

Life is full of choices. The choices we make affect our lives and the lives of those around us. Because God has given us a free will, we can choose to do right or wrong. We can choose to forgive or to not forgive.

Must you forgive others? No. You do not *have* to forgive other people. But ask yourself, "Is there anyone I *should* forgive with regard to my abortion?"

What does it mean to forgive others?

Before we discuss the why, who, and how of forgiveness, it will help to understand precisely what it means to forgive another person. The dictionary defines the word "forgive" as "To give up resentment against or the desire to punish; stop being angry with; pardon; 2. to give up all claim to punish or exact penalty for (an offense); overlook; 3. to cancel or remit (a debt)."[1]

Forgiveness is more than giving up resentment toward another person. Forgiveness is extending to that other person what God has done for you. Have you ever heard the story of the unforgiving servant? It's found in Matthew 18:21–35. A servant owed his master an enormous sum of money. He went to his master and begged to be forgiven the debt. His kind master forgave the debt. That same servant then went out and found a fellow slave who owed him money. The fellow slave could not pay the debt and begged for forgiveness. The slave, who had been forgiven of the large debt by his master, threw his fellow slave into prison. The master heard of this and rebuked the unforgiving servant, reminding him of the debt he had been forgiven. As a penalty for refusing to forgive a debt after the kindness showed to him, the master threw the unforgiving slave into prison. Forgiving means passing on to others the forgiveness extended through Christ to you.

Forgiveness has no limit. It has no contingencies. Forgiveness is understanding that it is not we who keep the records, but God. Forgiveness means never mentioning the incident again once you have settled it—not to the other person or to anyone else. It means not thinking about the incident. It

1. *Webster's New World Dictionary of the American Language,* College edition (The World Publishing Company, New York, 1966), p. 568.

means forgetting about it just as God has forgotten about your sin.

I believe forgiveness involves three factors. First, we must *understand in our mind* the necessity for forgiveness. Second, we must *choose with our will* to forgive. Third, our *heart must be aware of the emotional commitment* we are making. Forgiveness is love in action—a response to a need that only we can fulfill.

Whew! That sounds like an impossible task! You feel such anger and resentment inside toward the various people who "helped" you to abort your baby. How on earth can you give up those feelings? You can, you know. And although you may not feel like doing it, you will experience a freedom and release that defies expression once you take the step.

Why should I forgive?

There are several reasons why we should forgive others for their involvement in our abortions. God in Ephesians 4:32 gives us the most important reason why we should forgive others: "Be kind to one another, tender-hearted, forgiving each other, just as God in Christ also has forgiven you" (see also Colossians 3:13). If you asked God through Christ to forgive you for aborting your unborn baby, He did. Christ had to leave heaven and come to earth as a man to die on the cross in order for a perfect God to forgive imperfect people. Imagine what a sacrifice that was—to leave the glories of heaven for thirty-three years and then to die for someone else. And Christ never opened His mouth to defend Himself (Isaiah 53:7). He silently took the blame for sins He never committed. He never got angry with us, never hated us. Instead, as Christ hung on the cross, He said to God, "Father, forgive them; for they do not know what they are doing" (Luke 23:34). Now God tells us that just as Christ did that for us, so we should forgive others. Our part is much easier than Christ's, because we do not have to suffer and die in order to forgive someone. We forgive by an act of our will.

Another reason to forgive is that when we ask God to forgive our sins, it is with the understanding that we have already forgiven others. Part of the Lord's Prayer in Luke 11:4a reads, "Forgive us our sins, for we also forgive everyone who sins against us" (NIV). How can we possibly present ourselves before God Almighty if we have failed to forgive someone a lesser sin than the ones we have committed? I like the way Dr. James Dobson puts it: "Realize that *no* offense by another person could equal our guilt before God who has already forgiven us. We are obligated to show that same mercy to others."[2]

I found that once I forgave others, my eyes were opened to the fact that those people involved in the pro-abortion movement are human beings who are just as precious to God as the human beings who were aborted. Forgiving others made me realize that God through Christ wants to forgive all those involved in abortion. But people won't change their minds unless they first see something in you and in me that makes them want to switch to our point of view. Those who are pro-abortion must see, not only the love and concern we have for unborn babies, but also the love and concern we have for *them.* That doesn't mean we will cease speaking the truth that abortion is murder. It does mean we will learn to differentiate between loving the individual and hating the evil he or she does. That's how God deals with us. God loved and forgave us even though we killed an innocent human being created in His own image. He loves us but hates our sin.

Think about this. If a person came at you about something you had done wrong with hatred in his or her eyes and bitterness in his or her heart, how would you react? Even if you *knew* you were wrong, chances are you would deny the wrong and harden your heart against correction (Proverbs 18:19). A forgiving spirit allows us to effectively approach people in order to teach them the truth. My parents loved and forgave me long before I asked for their forgiveness. I

2. Dr. James Dobson, *Focus on the Family Bulletin,* March 1989.

had killed their grandchild—a blood-related part of them. The reason they forgave is that they loved me more than they hated my sin.

One reason to forgive is a very practical one—for your own health. I found an interesting article in *The Washington Times* which explains that people who fail to release anger often have heart problems caused by a chronic constriction of the blood vessels that reduce the flow of blood to the heart.[3] Think about it. It makes sense. Failure to forgive people causes bitterness to fester inside of us. If we remain tense, it affects us physiologically. On the other hand, "A joyful heart is good medicine" (Proverbs 17:22a).

A final reason for forgiving those who participated in your decision to have an abortion is that forgiveness is a release. It frees you from sin that keeps you bound. It releases that other person from being bound by your anger toward them. It opens the way for the Holy Spirit to work in both your lives. It releases you by breaking down the walls of enmity you have constructed.[4] Forgiveness sets you free!

Whom should I forgive?

You should forgive anyone personally involved in your abortion against whom you harbor feelings of anger, resentment, bitterness, hate, or animosity. You may have to do some serious thinking to come up with all the names of those you need to forgive. There may be some people against whom you've never consciously admitted holding a grudge. People to forgive might include your personal physician, the specific people who performed your abortion, your parents, boyfriend, or husband, and other relatives or friends. That same

3. John Accola, "Chronic Anger Found Hazardous to Heart," *The Washington Times,* January 10, 1989.
4. "Seven Steps to Healing," unsigned seminar notes from Open ARMs convention, May 1987.

forgiveness should be extended to those not personally involved in your abortion. This would include owners of abortion clinics, anyone who performs or assists in performing abortions, legislators who voted for liberal abortion laws, the Supreme Court which decided abortion was a woman's right, and various members of society who pushed for that right.

Let me give you an example of how many people some of us need to forgive. The following is quoted from a letter I received: "I'm angry with everyone—even God. I am a nurse. I see multiple women who have had one or more abortions and drop babies like rabbits. They have no income to support the children and most are unwed and drug addicts. Why am I being punished? I have a wonderful husband, job, home, and income. I'm truly sorry for my abortion—but that doesn't matter. I can't have a child. That hurts."

Can you pick out the people this woman needs to forgive? Although she is "angry with everyone," a blanket act of forgiveness will not do. She must specifically and individually forgive God, women who have aborted and can still bear children, pregnant women, women with children, people who are poor and have children, unmarried mothers, women who are addicted to drugs yet still have children, and herself. That's quite a few people, isn't it?

It helps to make a list of people you need to forgive. Wherever possible, use a person's specific name (e.g., "Dr. Jones" rather than simply "doctor"). It may take you a while, but write down every name. Ask God to bring names to mind. When I did this, some of the people who came up surprised me; I did not consciously realize I harbored ill feelings against them.

How do I forgive others?

We are down to the hard part. We have realized there are people we need to forgive. We have made a list either mentally or on paper of who those people are. Now we must

103

carry out our commitment to rid ourselves of the guilt we carry by not having forgiven people who hurt us. We must turn our hate list into a love list.

Charles Stanley, in his book *Forgiveness,* sets forth five steps which are involved in forgiving.

1. Recognize you are totally forgiven by God, and therefore can forgive others.
2. Release others from the debt you think they owe to you.
3. Release the other person from any responsibility to meet your needs.
4. View other people as God's tools for your growth and maturity.
5. Reconcile with those from whom you have been estranged.[5]

Reconciliation involves two actions: *seeking* forgiveness for wrongs done to others and *extending* forgiveness to those who seek pardon. A person who has hurt you may come to you to seek your forgiveness. In this instance, you should forgive them no matter what part they played in your abortion. The Bible tells us to forgive seventy times seven, which means we should forgive a person whenever they ask, no matter how many times they ask. Our task here is not to judge, but to keep on forgiving.

Usually people will not come to you. It will be your responsibility to go to them. There are several ways you can initiate a reconciliation. The best way (and the hardest) is to go to people in person to seek their forgiveness for your improper response to them. If distance is a problem, you may want to telephone or write to each person you need to forgive. In some cases you may not know how to contact a person. This often is the case with medical personnel or possibly the father of your baby. To this day I have been unable to

5. Charles Stanley, *Forgiveness* (Oliver Nelson, Division of Thomas Nelson Publishers, Nashville, 1987), pp. 127–130.

locate the father of my aborted baby. To rid myself of my anger toward him, I forgave him in my heart before God. Additionally, I pray for him and others that they may one day seek God's forgiveness for their part in my abortion.

You will want to speak privately and sincerely, with humility and love. Your words should include admission and acceptance of your responsibility for your abortion. This is such a good opportunity for these other people to see the change Christ has made in your life. Tell them that you have been wrong and want to set things right. Tell these people you forgive them for their participation in your abortion. Tell them that you have asked Christ to forgive your sin in aborting your unborn baby. Explain why you now understand it was wrong. Explain that because Christ forgave you, you now have the freedom and desire to forgive others. Then say these words: "I am sorry. Will you forgive me?" I know—the words will probably stick in your throat. You can do it. It won't be easy, but the reward will far surpass the difficulty!

Will I ever be able to forgive _____ for the part that person played in my abortion?

There may be that one person you believe you simply cannot forgive. The blank was left intentionally for you to mentally fill with that person's name. Who is it—your boyfriend, your mother, the clinic, Planned Parenthood? I know what you are feeling and how difficult forgiving will be.

Three biblical examples of forgiveness under the most difficult circumstances occur to me. The first is Joseph, who forgave his brothers although they had conspired to kill him and sold him into slavery, resulting in Joseph spending two years in prison for a crime he never committed.[6] Next consider Stephen, the first Christian martyr. As he was being stoned to death, he cried out, "Lord, do not hold this sin against them!" (Acts 7:60). Finally, I think of the Lord Jesus Christ,

6. Joseph's moving story is recorded in Genesis 37–50.

who, as He hung on the cross dying for my sins, pleaded, "Father, forgive them; for they do not know what they are doing" (Luke 23:34).

You *can* forgive that person. But you must choose by an act of your will to forgive him or her.

Why am I having such a difficult time forgiving others?

It's normal to struggle with forgiving others. You have been deeply hurt by people who influenced you to abort. Forgiving others is not a normal human response. It's okay for it to be hard. Forgiveness takes a superhuman effort. That is why it cannot be accomplished without God's intervention. God gives our heart the love which enables us to honestly and completely forgive others. Don't try to forgive in your own strength, because you will find it impossible and/or temporary. The quotation which reads, "To err is human, to forgive divine" has much truth to it.

A personal story from the life of Corrie ten Boom reveals the difficulty in forgiving others. In 1947 Corrie ten Boom, a former prisoner at Ravensbruck concentration camp, had returned to defeated Germany bringing the message that God forgives. Present in the auditorium was a man who had been a guard during Miss ten Boom's incarceration. She remembered him. At the end of her message, this man came forward and said that he had now become a Christian. He knew that God had forgiven him, but he wanted to know if Miss ten Boom would also forgive him. This he asked of a woman who daily lived and spoke God's forgiveness. Yet for Miss ten Boom time stood still as she fought her strong desire to not touch her former guard's hand in forgiveness. Scenes of her sister's death and the humiliations she herself endured at Ravensbruck leaped to mind. Corrie ten Boom knew forgiveness is not an emotion, but rather an act of the will. She knew the will could function "regardless of the temperature of the heart." She silently prayed for Jesus to help her. She lifted her hand as she asked God to supply the feeling. She mechanically thrust her hand into the hand of her former guard. Corrie ten Boom relates that she experienced a healing warmth which extended from her shoulder down through their joined hands. With tears in her eyes she cried out "I forgive you, brother!" Miss ten Boom says she never knew God's love more intensely than at that moment.[7]

A terrible wrong has been done to you by others. You won't correct the situation by inflicting more wrong on those people by words or actions. Instead, display love and forgiveness. With God's help, you can and will forgive every person involved with your abortion.

How should I respond to those who reject my forgiveness?

Sometimes we want to place a contingency upon the forgiveness we extend to others. This is that phase of grieving called bargaining. If we forgive others, we expect others to forgive us. This is a normal expectation. However, if the people we seek forgiveness from refuse to forgive us—what then? Do we retract our words until those people come around? No, we forgive them for their sins. We understand that the problem is now between them and God. Perhaps this little acrostic will help:

*F*or
*O*nce
*R*ealize
*G*od
*I*s
*V*indicating
*E*verything!

7. Corrie ten Boom, *I'm Still Learning to Forgive* (Good News Publishers, Westchester, Illinois, n.d.), tract.

What if I choose not to forgive?

There is no gentle way to put this. If you do not do what God tells you to do, if you do not extend to others the forgiveness God has given to you, you will not heal. Period. The fact is, if you refuse to forgive, or hold contingencies upon forgiving, then you will continue to suffer. Your anger, bitterness, and frustration will build up until you either explode with rage or become eaten up with self-pity.

Alma wrote these words: "This letter does not come easy. I am learning to let it be easy for it is not my burden anymore. I have spoken to my husband (who does not know Jesus as his Lord) and asked his forgiveness for it was my strong stand that made our choices. I have also written to my parents asking their forgiveness. They have not talked to me about it, but I am free of the burden. I may never get them to speak to me face to face. But, I feel free from the years of pain and emotional turmoil."

Laura writes, "One day the Lord spoke to me regarding forgiving the doctor, Planned Parenthood and others involved in my abortion. He said, 'Forgive them for they know not what they are doing.' I realized then that they thought they were helping me. They used words like 'menstrual extraction' because they felt an uninformed decision was a less painful one. They only added to my denial—I wish they had been honest; but I chose to forgive them with the Lord's help. This is one of the ways I was able to be free." That same freedom will be yours once you forgive all those involved in your abortion. The choice is yours. What will you do?

CHAPTER THIRTEEN

Will I Be Punished for My Abortion?

"I suffered severe baby blues until I found out I was pregnant again, then I carried my daughter in utter guilt expecting God to punish me for my previous abortion."

Christine

Aborted women have committed murder. We struggle with the knowledge that, because of the method chosen, the murder was legal. Therefore, no investigation, trial, or conviction by a court of law will ever occur. We *know* we committed murder—yet society declares we merely terminated a pregnancy. We *know* we are guilty—yet society declares we are innocent of any crime. We *know* we deserve punishment —yet society declares there *was* no crime.

Because we understand that we committed murder, our conscience desires retribution to satisfy the guilt. We believe with all our hearts we *deserve* punishment. But we will never experience punishment from society. If not society, then from whom? Our minds quickly respond, "God, of course!"

Is God punishing me?

This question implies that God *is* punishing you. Women asking this question invariably view the punisher as God, the cause of the punishment their abortion, and the recipient themselves or their loved ones. People generally view punishment, not as a consequence of their own actions, but as judgment passed upon them by another. For instance, a child refuses to obey his mother. Mother spanks him. The child sees his mother as a condemning judge. However, although the punishment is *carried out* by the mother, it results as a *consequence* of wrong action on the part of the child. Mother spanks to correct wrong behavior.

Love and concern for another's well-being demands that discipline be done following incorrect behavior. I sometimes tell my children before I discipline them, "This will hurt me more than it will hurt you." That's true! It hurts me terribly to cause my children any pain. However, because I love them, I discipline them in order to get their attention and focus it on the fact that there *is* a problem which needs correcting. This idea of some type of punishment to correct behavior is the brainchild not of any person but of God. God has chastised people since the Garden of Eden incident when Adam and Eve ate the forbidden fruit and were evicted from the garden.

The key concept to grasp here is that punishment from God is not against us. It is against disobedience to His Word. God always punishes unrepentant sin in order to bring us to repentance and restoration. God disciplines us as a father would his children. Once we choose to correct our wrong action and obey, God no longer "spanks" us (Hebrews 12:5–11). Although *natural* consequences of our actions may result, these are not punishment from God. Be assured, God does *not* sit in heaven looking for ways to punish you for your abortion.

Is there a reason God might still punish me?

God punishes only unrepentant sin. Examine your life. Are you habitually doing anything of which God would disapprove? If so, you are in danger of being chastised.

Let me give you an example of a specific sin God would punish if not confessed and repented of: Since approximately 80 percent of abortions are performed on unmarried women, most of us were involved in fornication (sexual relationship outside of marriage) at the time we became pregnant. We got caught at an untimely moment. We were surprised. We had thought, "It will never happen to me." We worried about the pregnancy to the point of having an abortion. Yet most of us never gave a second thought to the fornication that resulted in the pregnancy. The fact is, if we had not been involved in fornication, pregnancy would not have occurred, and therefore abortion would never have been considered or chosen.

God forbids fornication. In Old Testament times, death by stoning was the penalty for fornication. However, in our modern age, sex outside of marriage is the norm. People are no longer ostracized (let alone stoned to death) for living together without a marriage license. But punishment for fornication still exists. The difference is that now it is the innocent unborn children along with their mothers who pay the price.

Often fear causes us to turn to God and to do right. Once that fear passes, our natural inclination is to return to our old ways. Following an abortion, many women return to the very lifestyle that led to pregnancy. Yet fear should continue to be very real because God *will* punish those who continue to commit fornication: "Marriage is honorable in all, and the bed undefiled: but whoremongers and adulterers God will judge" (Hebrews 13:4 KJV).

Some sin will not be easy to give up. We may enjoy it. Our deceitful heart tells us, "Aw, go ahead, God won't punish you for this." What we need to say is "Lord, I'm wrong. You are right. With your help, I will choose to obey."

How does abortion affect my chances of conceiving another child?

This is a frequently asked question. Because we have lost one baby so tragically, the thought of not being able to have another burdens our mind. Do you find yourself thinking about the following?

• Is there hope of bearing future children? I've read it's hard to get pregnant after an abortion. I have been trying for nine months to get pregnant. I don't know if the problem is stress, guilt, past infection, or past abortion. Not knowing is the worst part. We plan to get it checked out soon.
• Could psychosomatic illness because of guilt over abortion prevent me from getting pregnant again?
• How will this affect my childbearing ability?
• I'm afraid I'll never be able to have more children.
• Will I be able to have children without any problems? Normal children?
• Am I to never have a child of my own? Is this the punishment?

Many criteria are involved in becoming pregnant. Conception can only occur during certain days of your monthly cycle. Your husband and you must both be fertile. Illness can inhibit your becoming pregnant. Then too, your mind is very powerful and can control certain bodily functions. Guilt and fear are two culprits. Our bodies work as a complete unit—mentally, physiologically, emotionally, and spiritually. When any one of these is out of kilter, a pregnancy could be blocked.

112

If you can't get pregnant, see your doctor and find out if there is a medical reason. If both you and your husband are fertile, try to relax during sex. Being "uptight" may keep conception from occurring. Ask your physician for other suggestions on increasing the likelihood of conception.

Why am I frightened of another pregnancy?

Any pregnancy causes concern to the extent that we hope for a healthy baby and anticipate changes in our lives as we assume new and awesome responsibilities. After all, babies come to us without an instruction manual!

However, following an abortion, women often find their apprehension heightened. This is normal. You may still have unresolved conflicts about your abortion. You have lost a child during pregnancy. He died because you aborted him, and you may believe God will punish you by allowing something to go wrong with a future pregnancy.

Following my abortion, I feared pregnancy. I feared I would not be able to become pregnant, and when I did, I feared God would punish me by allowing my baby to be deformed. When Michael was born perfect in every way, I accepted the fact that God would *not* punish me in this way.

As I came to understand God's ways better, I realized that had one of my children been born handicapped or deformed, that would not indicate God had punished me or my child. God permits people to be formed as they are for a reason—so that the glory of God may be seen in their lives (John 9:3; Exodus 4:11). If you should bear a "special" child, thank God for the baby, and ask Him to help you and the child know His purpose.

Would God try to punish me by letting something happen to my other children?

Just as God does not punish your future children, so He would not punish your living children to "get back" at you. God loves you and your children. He wants only the best for you and them. You believe that, don't you? Then grab hold of it and hang on! "For God has not given us the spirit of fear; but of power, and of love, and of a sound mind" (2 Timothy 1:7). If you fear that God will "do something" to your living children in order to punish you, your life will be spent in pessimistic expectation. The only child punished by your abortion was the baby you aborted.

How can you forgive yourself for any future problem pregnancies that may occur (miscarriage, stillbirth, etc.)? How do you handle the grief and guilt when you realize that the abortion may have affected this?

Problems in future pregnancies *can* occur as a result of your abortion. But they are a natural consequence and not related to God punishing you.

If you are living with a difficult situation resulting from your abortion, I understand how you feel. My daughter Sarah is a surviving twin. I miscarried her fraternal brother or sister during my third month of pregnancy. Whether or not the miscarriage was a direct consequence of my abortion I will never know. I *do* know that wallowing in grief and guilt won't correct the problem and would only lead me to further despair. I find it helps to ask God how He wants to use such a situation to help me or another person to grow stronger.

God wants to meet your need. It's foolish to try to cope with our feelings on our own. An anonymous woman writes, "I thought time would heal the wounds that I self-inflicted,

114

but it only made it worse. I had a miscarriage a few years after and felt I was receiving just payment. I thought God took a life since I did. Then I turned to Jesus Christ and received forgiveness from this horrible sin. Now I have peace and comfort to make it through the day that only God can offer." This woman has learned to cast her burdens on Jesus (Psalms 55:22). His shoulders are broad and strong. Jesus wants to bear *your* burdens. Won't you let Him?

What if I can't have other children?

There are women throughout the world that yearn to bear a child and cannot. Not all of these women have experienced abortion. If your abortion has resulted in sterility, your pain must be great. I know getting pregnant is probably the most important thing to you at this point in your life. Try to keep it in perspective. You can have a fulfilling life without children, but you must choose to do so and set your mind in that direction.

Because I believe God can do anything, I want you to know something. I personally know four women who wanted desperately to become pregnant. All four were medically determined to be barren. Through intervention of prayer, two of these women now have children. Yes, these were miracles. Our God is the God of miracles. Two women still remain barren. For whatever His reason, God chose to deny these women the children they so desire. Although people perform the act that can result in conception, God opens and closes the womb. Julie's words carry much wisdom: "Someday I'll get married and will want to have children. It often scares me that I won't be able to. But the Lord will be there to comfort me. I don't know what His plans are for me, but they will be in His will."

If you cannot have children, you may want to consider adoption. Because of your experience, your capacity to love may have been enlarged. Phyllis Lefort wrote this acrostic:

A		*A*
*B*aby		*D*amsel
*O*rdered		*O*pposing
*R*emoved		*P*regnancy
*T*ransmits	vs.	*T*houghtfully
*I*nnocent		*I*nitiates
*O*utcries		*O*ffspring's
*N*obody hears		*N*ext home

Perhaps God has chosen you to provide a home for a baby to whom a young girl has chosen to give life.

I'm still single in my thirties. Is God punishing me?

Most questions related to punishment following an abortion focus on children. However, one woman asked the question just posed. For a woman who wants very much to marry and raise a family, this can be a tormenting question. You may believe God sees you as unfit to marry and mother another child. Again, God will not punish you for your abortion by keeping you unmarried. Sometimes there is a very logical reason why a woman remains single. The woman who asked this question recently married. She responds this way: "Now I know that singleness later [in life] is a product of our generation and of accepting the world's view of what is fulfilling for a woman."

We do not know the future, but God does. Remaining single may be His perfect plan for you. On the other hand, God's timing is perfect. Perhaps this very minute your future husband is looking for *you!*

116

How do I deal with or lose the feeling that someday I am going to "pay" for this?

We feel so bad about our abortion that we can't believe the punishment we so justly deserve won't follow. We want the release that punishment will bring, and at the same time we fear what the punishment will be.

You may still feel guilty about your abortion. We must not live our lives in accordance with our guilty feelings. Feelings can err, mislead, and confuse. Guilt often causes us to run in an attempt to escape impending punishment. In the Bible, Moses ran when he had killed the Egyptian; Jonah ran after refusing to obey God; David killed Uriah to hide his sin of adultery with Bathsheba. In all three cases these people were found out, punished, and, at their request, reconciled to God once more.

The Bible admonishes, "Be sure your sin will find you out." Your sin *did* find you out—your conscience revealed it to you—and you were punished until you repented. Some natural consequences of having had an abortion may include the inability to bear or carry more children. Infections and other medical problems may occur. Even though some of the consequences of your abortion may remain throughout your life, you are forgiven for the sin of abortion once you choose to trust Christ as your Savior.

The punishment you should have had for your abortion has been negated by the laws of our land. One woman writes, "God has been so good to us and I really can't understand it. If things were as they should be I should be in prison with a life sentence or even have already been executed." God has not dealt with us according to our sin. God is just but He is also sovereign. In His sovereignty He chooses to be merciful to those who love and obey Him. The punishment we deserved was spared us. Yet a crime was committed and someone must pay. Someone has. His name is Jesus.

CHAPTER FOURTEEN

Where Is My Baby Now?

"I have assurance that Jesus is caring for my baby and has been all along."

Phyllis Lefort

I want to believe *my* baby is in heaven. Every aborted woman I have ever spoken with believes *her* baby is in heaven. Is there any biblical support for our belief?

As I've struggled with the destiny of aborted babies, I knew I would eventually be called upon to speak or write on this most important issue. This is that time and this is what I believe.

What did they do with my baby?

Many women have written with concerns over the physical disposal of their babies. Wondering if the baby was used for "spare parts" or research troubles some women. My own aborted baby was disposed of like a piece of garbage. I know, because I watched the nurse carry his tiny body to the disposal, and I listened as they flushed him down. That was harder to live through than I could ever put into words. But since that time many years ago, I have come to realize an important fact. It does not matter what happened to the physical remains of your baby. God, who created the world and all that is in it, can easily "put back together" a body torn apart by human hands. What matters is what happened to his soul—that part which lives on after the physical body dies.

Does God recognize the unborn baby as a person?

In order for us to better understand God's view of the unborn, it will help to look at His words.

God knew us prior to birth:

> For Thou didst form my inward parts; Thou didst weave me in my mother's womb. I will give thanks to Thee, for I am fearfully and wonderfully made; Wonderful are Thy works, And my soul knows it very well. My frame was not hidden from Thee, When I was made in secret, And skillfully wrought in the depths of the earth. Thine eyes have seen my unformed substance; And in Thy book they were all written, The days that were ordained for me, When as yet there was not one of them. (Psalms 139:13–16)

Thus says the Lord, your Redeemer, and the one who formed you from the womb, I, the Lord, and the maker of all things. (Isaiah 44:24a)

Before I formed you in the womb I knew you. (Jeremiah 1:5a)

Normal human actions occur in the womb:

In the womb he [Jacob] took his brother [Esau] by the heel. (Hosea 12:3a)

And it came about that when Elizabeth heard Mary's greeting, the baby leaped in her womb. (Luke 1:41a, 44)

God places a high value on the life of the tiny person you carried in your womb. Unique and created in God's own image, he was of inestimable value to God. Because God sees the end from the beginning, God saw your baby as a person before he was formed.

God refers to unborn babies and born children with the same word, the term *brephos* in the Greek. Children are so highly valued by Jesus that He told his disciples not to hinder their coming to Him. Yes, God recognizes the unborn as human beings.

Does an unborn baby have a soul?

Philosophers and theologians have speculated through the ages on the soul and its origin (ensoulment)—before conception, at conception, at birth, or somewhere in between. I believe ensoulment occurs at conception.

When God first formed Adam's body, God breathed into him and man became a living soul (Genesis 2:7). Our soul is as much a part of us as our body. Our body permits us to function on this earth, to relate to other people and things.

120

Our soul permits us to relate to God. It lives on after our body dies. Without a soul a human being is dead (James 2:26).[1] Therefore, if an unborn human baby did not have a soul, it would not be alive. We know that the unborn *do* live. God declares it. We have seen it. Since human life exists in the womb, then he has a soul from the moment he comes into existence—at conception. Yes, your baby, no matter how small, has a soul.

Is my aborted baby in heaven?

Abortion ends God's plan for the baby's life on earth. We know the body is disposed of, but what happens to his soul? This opens the door to some sobering thoughts. If all babies go to heaven, why not abort *all* babies to insure they spend eternity with God? The answer is that the end never justifies the means. More importantly, God determines the length of one's life. If only some go to heaven, it behooves us to think carefully before conceiving children or aborting them, for we may have sentenced a human being to hell.

As I consider this question, John 3:3–7 stands out clearly in my mind. This passage tells us that a person must be born again—once from the mother and once from the Holy Spirit. Romans 6 tells us *all* are in sin. David states that his mother conceived him in sin (Psalms 51:5).[2] If you have ever seen a small baby throw a temper tantrum, you can easily believe the truth of this! You and I must choose to receive Christ to be forgiven our sins, but an *unborn* baby has never chosen to sin. Not only that, but he was never born a first time and so could not choose to be "born again"!

Deuteronomy 1:39 states, "Moreover, your little ones who

1. No scriptural support exists for the concept that souls exist prior to conception.
2. This refers not to his mother sinning during the act of conception, but to the fact that David was in a state of sin *from* conception.

121

you said would become a prey, and your sons, who this day have no knowledge of good or evil, shall enter there [the promised land], and I will give it to them, and they shall possess it." Although this passage refers to Israel inheriting the promised land, the implication is clear: children were not held responsible for the sin of their parents. Some people apply this passage to aborted babies, believing it indicates that God will not hold aborted babies responsible for their mothers' sin of abortion.

Other passages confirm God's faithfulness to His children:

For my father and my mother have forsaken me, But the Lord will take me up. (Psalms 27:10)

Can a nursing woman forget her nursing child, and have no compassion on the son of her womb? Even these may forget, but I [God] will not forget you. (Isaiah 49:15)

To vindicate the orphan and the oppressed, That man who is of the earth may cause terror no more. (Psalms 10:18)

When we aborted, we relinquished the opportunity to know whether our child would come to trust Christ as his personal Savior. Although the Bible does not come out and say in so many words, "Aborted babies are in heaven," we can believe with assurance that God is in control and has done what is right.

Will I ever see my baby again?

The classic passage which infers that dead babies are with the Lord and we will one day join them is found in 2 Samuel 12:23b. David says at the death of his baby, "I shall go to him, but he will not return to me." The inference is clear— one day David expects to see his child in heaven.

Some things are hard to understand and/or accept. God's

idea of what is "fair" is based on His infinite and all-knowing mind. Our idea of what is "fair" is limited to our understanding of what happens to us and to those around us. God is merciful *and* just. What He chooses to do is acceptable to me.

Worrying is wrong because we don't know. Nothing we can do now will alter or clarify our hope. Yet it is right to hope *because* we don't know. Hebrews 11:1 tells us faith is the substance of things hoped for.[3] Read the words of women who are secure in the hope of one day reuniting with their babies:

> I believe that my baby is in heaven now. There is a picture in an Open ARMs pamphlet that helps a lot. It is a picture of Jesus holding a baby in His arms. It always gives me comfort, and helps me to know that I will see my child some day, and that even he/she has forgiven me for taking his/her life away. I don't know in what form he/she will be in, but I know that I will recognize him/her and love him/her like I've never loved before. (Stephanie)

> Their bodies were probably disposed of, like trash. But their souls are with their Creator. I see now that God twice offered me the most precious and valuable gift He ever made. Instead of being thankful and appreciative, I took His gifts and ruined them; but such is His mercy and love, that I know I need not fear His rebuke for my ingratitude—I believe He and they, my first two babies, will be waiting to welcome me into heaven when my life on earth ends. (Regina)

> I believe that child is in heaven with the Lord; that he is whole and happy. I believe that He would want me to be happy and that I will meet him someday—we will be reunited. "Let the children come to me, do not hinder

3. "Hope" in this context refers to the secure belief that something *will* happen, coupled with a longing for it *to* happen.

them, for the kingdom of heaven is made up of such as these." I had to release him to the Father's care. (Laura)

We only torture ourselves by dwelling on the past and worrying about the future. To function normally, we must concentrate on the present. I do not worry about my baby, or about seeing him again—he is in God's hands now. I do think of seeing Jesus. I concentrate, not on seeing my baby, but on one day seeing God who has forgiven me. I long to see Jesus.

Will we recognize them in heaven?

First Corinthians 15:35–56 tells us we will receive a new and wonderfully different body at the resurrection. Glorified. Incorruptible. Imperishable. Powerful. The old body was human in appearance and actions. The new body will be like Christ—perfect in every way. Whether the body will be in the form of a baby or an adult, no one knows. Jesus Himself was not instantly recognized following His resurrection. But once He revealed His identity, people recognized Him as the one they had loved and lost and had now regained.

An anonymous woman penned this poem to express her conviction:

Where Is My Baby?

Sitting here by the ocean
I reflect upon my abortion

The child that once
Could have laughed and sang
Won't ever be here again.

My arms ache to hold her
The babe so sweet
Hold her all morning
Hold her all week.

My arms are now empty
Along with my heart
When I think of the time
And moments apart

I wonder how close
The two of us
Would have been
Mother, baby,
Child and friend

I love you my darling
Tho this moment in time
I can't see or talk to you
Or say you are mine

When I reflect upon it all
I think of my baby cuddly and small

I know my child is with the Lord
Held in the arms of the Savior I adore
Who I ask you, could ask for more?

Someday I'll see my child so sweet
And then everything will be complete.

CHAPTER FIFTEEN

Should I Tell My Baby Good-bye?

"I felt I couldn't say good-bye until I had said hello—I asked the Lord to reveal to me the sex of my child. Then I named him. It gave me a sense of closure to be able to pray to the Lord about Joseph. . . ."

Donna Merrick

In our culture we practice specific rituals as part of the grieving process following a death. To tell our loved one good-bye, we lay the body out for viewing, send flowers, gather family and friends together to comfort us, recount actions and attributes of the deceased, conduct a memorial service, and finally bury our dead.

With abortion, culture dictates we "ignore" the death as though it had never occurred. Those of us who have aborted face a dilemma. We desire to formally close this chapter of our lives, yet there is no prescribed and accepted method by which we may accomplish this act of "saying good-bye." What are we to do?

Is it normal for me to desire reconciliation with my baby?

The fact that you want to make things right with your aborted baby indicates you are truly repentant of your action. Many women, knowing they caused their own baby's death, feel as you do. You may have sought forgiveness from those you wronged when you aborted, and now this one "hurdle" remains before you lay the baby to rest within your mind. You want to complete the cycle of restoration with this most intimately involved person.

The thought of reconciliation with the baby makes us feel better. Reconciliation means to settle an account or to resolve a situation. The baby lived and died without our knowing him or her. He really existed but was unknown to us. Thus, when we speak of reconciliation with our dead baby, we refer to the act of settling things *in our own mind.* The desire for "making it right" with your baby is not wrong. The method you select to accomplish that reconciliation must be carefully considered and chosen.

Does my child forgive me for what I've done?

On the one hand, women look forward to one day seeing their aborted child in heaven, while on the other, they fear that same child will not forgive them. The fear is real but the object of that fear is imagined. Just as, in an old house which creaks and moans, we can believe in our minds someone is prowling, so we can believe our dead baby is capable of hate or malice toward us. The truth is, there is no prowler. Likewise, the baby is not waiting to avenge his death. But imagination can easily become reality to us if we focus on it long enough. Trust these words from Ecclesiastes 9:5–6: "For the living know they will die; but the dead do not know

127

anything, nor have they any longer a reward, for their memory is forgotten. Indeed their love, their hate, and their zeal have already perished, and they will no longer have a share in all that is done under the sun."

The attempt to seek forgiveness from your dead baby is a way of dealing with your grief and guilt. You may have acknowledged guilt in murdering your child, but "it is another thing to come face to face with [your] victim, the one [you] have hurt. [You] must come to a point of peace with the aborted child, trusting that, before God, [you] have done all [you] could do to right [your] wrong."[1]

Sometimes women seem more concerned about the baby forgiving them than about reconciling wrongs committed against living people. We need to keep this in perspective. We have seen that God tells us to seek forgiveness from those we have wronged. Always this command refers to living people. Never are we told to reconcile with the dead. There is *no need* for you to seek the baby's forgiveness or to worry if he will forgive you.

Fearing your baby keeps you in bondage. Jesus has made all things right, and you should anticipate one day giving your child a heavenly hug.

I want so desperately to communicate my feelings to my baby. Why?

The thought of communicating with your baby gives substance to the "ghost" of a wished-for memory. We want to let the baby know he was loved, to hold for a moment that baby in our arms, to tell him we are sorry. Our mothering instinct, fueled by our guilt, seeks to reach completion for a relationship hastily cut off.

You may vocally express the fact that your abortion killed

1. Debbie Marshall and Patti Goodoien, *In His Image: A Post-abortion Bible Study,* leader's guide (Open ARMs, Indianapolis, 1989), p. 46.

an unborn human being. Yet you may find the mental knowledge has no emotional reality for you. In order to help you come to grips with this, someone may encourage you to hold a doll and tell it what you want your baby to hear. A doll cannot provide the fulfillment you seek. Fantasizing merely creates a dangerous illusion.

Although the desire to express your feelings to the baby is normal, you must come to understand that those same feelings are one-sided because the baby is beyond the emotions and reactions of mortals.

Hebrews 11:1 tells us faith is the evidence of things not seen. Faith in the unseen Christ allows God to forgive us all our sins. Faith that God is caring for that child without our ever having seen him permits us to let the baby "rest in peace." We can continue on with our lives secure in the hope of future actual reconciliation.

Trying to establish a relationship with your dead baby will hinder your healing because you are refusing to accept your baby's death. Relinquish that child to God's care.

What are the methods for saying good-bye?

Suggested methods fall under two categories: *Physical actions* include writing letters, holding memorial services, and using dolls as baby substitutes. *Mental exercises* include assigning attributes such as sex, hair color, or features, giving the baby a name and birth date, and visualization. Each method serves as an aid for you to use to reconcile your abortion experience *in your own mind.* The intent is good—to help you close this chapter of your life. However, the benefits of most of the procedures are doubtful, while other procedures are downright harmful.

What would my child have been like had I not had an abortion?

People have distinct identities and attributes. Questions regarding the physical attributes of your unborn baby are normal. Would it have been a boy or a girl? Would it have looked like you or the father? What color would his hair have been? When would he have been born? You may believe that knowing will draw you closer to your child, give you a sense of closure, make the baby more real.

You can convince yourself of virtually anything. You may even *feel* better, but that doesn't indicate the problems have been dealt with and resolved, because feelings are not always accurate indicators of true healing. For instance, you can absolutely convince yourself your baby was a boy. You can believe it. You can name "him." To you, your baby *was* a boy. In reality it may have been a girl. The fantasy is real for you. But the reality is contrary to the fantasy. The reality is, you may not know the sex of your aborted baby. Period. Why spend time and energy creating an illusion that cannot help and will only harm you in the long run?

The truth is, knowing what your child would have been like is not possible. One of the consequences of abortion is that it negates your having a relationship with your child on this earth. Many women feel the need to assign physical attributes and birth dates to their aborted babies. Fantasizing his physical attributes or personality can only keep the baby alive in your mind. Part of our loss is *not* knowing the details of our baby's appearance and personality. What you need to do is trust God and ask Him to put these questions *from* your mind.

Should I name my baby?

Many women find naming their baby helps to identify him in their own mind as a "real" person. Because the baby is dead, a name does not matter to the baby. My baby has a name only because I carried him for nearly six months prior to the abortion and had selected a name for a baby to whom I had anticipated giving live birth. I never think of him by name. Please be careful you don't use his name to keep your child alive in your mind. It is right that his memory should fade gradually and naturally.

Did you know God has named your baby? Revelation 2:17 says, ". . . I will give him a white stone, and a new name written on the stone which no one knows but he who receives it." Doesn't it excite you to think your precious baby already has a God-given name!

Will writing a letter to my baby help?

Many women write letters to their baby as an aid to help them grieve outwardly. Writing letters also helps fulfill the need to "get it right" with someone who has died and to whom you cannot communicate your regret regarding his or her death. How many times have we wished we had said something, or done something, to or for people while they lived? At their death we regret our acts of omission and commission done during their life. However, once the person is gone, we have lost our opportunity to set right the wrongs.

If you have trusted Christ as your Savior, God has forgiven you for those wrongs. Although people in heaven may be able to "tune in" to earthly activities, you must not view your letter as a direct communication with your dead baby. Consciously seeking to communicate with the dead is forbidden by God (Deuteronomy 18:10–13), and Satan will use this to keep you in bondage. If you write the letter merely to get your feelings out, then I would say go ahead.

If you choose to pour out your feelings regarding the wrong you did to your unborn baby in a letter, just keep in mind that a letter won't change things. Just as a word spoken in anger can never be retracted, so our abortions, done in selfishness and/or fear, can never be undone. Apologies can be extended but the wrong can never be undone. It is essential to realize the letter expresses thoughts you *wish* you had been able to share with your baby. Why not write the letter to God instead, telling Him what you want your baby to know?

Does visualization help?

Caution must be exercised in our use of the term "visualization." Synonymous terms include "channeling" and "guided imagery." This imagery, which the New Age movement advocates, is based on imagination. Visualization is used to "get you in touch with your feelings." New Agers believe a positive mental image of a particular problem will promote healing through the power of consciousness. The action is entirely voluntary and self-induced. You think consciously in your mind of something you want very much to happen, and then you "visualize" that event taking place (e.g., you may be asked to "visualize" yourself holding your baby).

New Agers view thought as the basis of reality. Visualization is a technique used to attempt to bring into being something that does not exist or to get something you want without effort on your part. People will tell you it works. It may *appear* to work, but in reality you are covering your problems with layers of false well-being, because New Age visualization is based upon your *personal* experiences and feelings. It is dangerous to you because the entire experience is based upon feelings, which are often unreliable. In order to heal, we must take steps based upon the Word of God which stands on its own *without* our personal experiences tacked on. God is the absolute basis of reality. Heed these words: "We are destroying speculations and every lofty thing raised up against the knowledge of God, and we are taking every thought captive to the obedience of Christ" (2 Corinthians 10:5).

Because the New Age movement sounds so good, so satisfying, so easy, we can become caught up in it without realizing that the techniques it advocates lead to self-destruction. New Age imagery produces false hope and is extremely dangerous, because if you "visualize" long enough, your mind will eventually accept falsehood as truth and fantasy as reality. You don't need to imagine anything to receive emotional healing. The Word of God promises healing to all who ask (Matthew 21:22).

Does God ever "show" women their babies?

Several women have written to me explaining that while in deep prayer they were presented with a "vision" of their child, sometimes in Jesus' arms or holding His hands. Wendy shares this:

> I was in the chapel praying when I suddenly had a picture in my mind. My Lord and Savior was standing on a path and He was wearing a long white robe. With one hand He held the hand of a young girl and with the other the hand of a younger boy. The non-condemning look of assurance I received from Christ and the waving by the children as they turned to go hand in hand with Jesus broke me in repentance of my selfish acts. And this "vision" was the beginning of my healing. It has taken time (as I believe most healing does) and I don't know if I'll ever be all the way through the woods—but I am no longer crippled! Praise God!

I see several key components in what Wendy says. First, her "vision" was spontaneous. Second, no attempt was made to communicate with the dead children. Finally, the "vision" served as a tool to repentance because it focused Wendy's mind on the enormity of her abortions.

Because God works uniquely in each believer's life, He may choose to give a particular person a spontaneous vision of a particular situation. The important thing to recognize is that a vision from God would never contradict or add to Scripture. Remember that Satan desires to deceive you and can appear as an angel of light. He imitates God, with one subtle and vital difference. Whenever Satan is at work, some part of what he advocates will contain a lie. Satan will always try to create doubt in a person's mind with respect to God's Word. Compare what you have seen in a "vision" with what God declares to be true in His Word. If there is a discrepancy, your "vision" was not from God.

Also, be aware of the fact that your own sincere yearning to "see" your aborted baby may cause your mind to present you with a "vision" of your heart's desire. I believe much of what women are experiencing comes from this latter situation. It is vital you do not focus your attention nor base your healing on receiving "visions."

What about having a memorial service?

A memorial service is held in order to commit to memory someone we have known and loved and is now gone from us through death. That means we fully realize he is dead and we choose not to continue to dwell on him, but only to recall him occasionally when something triggers a memory which shoots to the foreground of our mind. Many men and women participate in memorial services for the purpose of giving dignity to aborted babies. Only you can decide if this activity will help you "bury" *your* baby.

Is there a method you recommend?

We have found we can only reconcile our grief *caused* by our abortions. We can never reconcile with the baby himself. We are alive. The child is dead. Reconciliation can only be accomplished between two living people. Seeking and extending forgiveness is an act requiring two people. It is not necessary to reconcile with your aborted baby. Nor is it possible. You must accept the fact that you did something irreparable in your eyes, but fully forgiven by God.

The concept of an aborted woman saying good-bye to her baby has focused on getting in touch with her thoughts and feelings regarding her baby in order to promote inner healing. This has become confused with reconciliation (the act of settling differences between living people), leaving the aborted woman grabbing at clouds of misconception. Continually focusing inwardly on various aspects of our abortion experience or the baby signals danger. We already know how horrendous our act was. Assigning characteristics to your baby or visualizing him causes you to form "memories" which are not part of reality but exist only in your mind. Additionally, focusing conscious attention on a specific event can make the memory more graphic and less accurate. We aborted women must learn to live without our child. Constant reminders and identifications hinder this goal. Rather than focusing on our inner selves, we must learn to focus on the God who loves and can heal us. True inner healing results from outward obedience to God's Word.

You may have utilized some of the methods described here. They may have served as a crutch, permitting you to function in a somewhat normal manner until the wound healed and you could once again walk on your own. But the crutch itself will never heal the wound. Only treatment by the Great Physician, Jesus Christ, and passage of time will do that.

I believe the best method of saying good-bye is to pray to God, seeking His forgiveness and committing the child to His care. Allow God to comfort you and give you peace. "Be anxious for nothing, but in everything by prayer and supplication with thanksgiving let your requests be made known to God. And the peace of God, which surpasses all comprehension, shall guard your hearts and your minds in Christ Jesus" (Philippians 4:6–7). The baby is gone. You are still alive and need to close this chapter of your life. If you desire, whisper a final "I'm sorry," then release your baby to God.

Nancy Berger wrote this poem, which expresses so well the proper attitude in closing this chapter of our lives:

In Memory of a Child

Dear Jesus,

I would so much like to know
The little life I took long ago.

Was the little one a girl or boy?
Does my child now bring you joy?

Never to see them laugh or hear them cry
Oh Jesus, they didn't deserve to die.

If someone had told me
About the child inside,
The little one would never have died.

I only thought about what I would do;
I didn't know my child had feeling too.

There is an emptiness deep inside,
And many nights I've [lain] and cried.

I cry for the child I will never see
Until you, Jesus, come for me.

If my child can see from up above
I hope my child will see my love.

The love I withheld so long ago
Was only because I didn't know.

So, Dear Jesus, I want to say,
Watch over my child until the day
The day when I can finally see,
That little child you gave to me.[2]

2. Nancy Berger, 1984.

CHAPTER SIXTEEN

Will I Ever Be Able to Forgive Myself?

"I know that I can't change the past, but I can certainly change the future. I want to live the rest of my life free from guilt and I believe God wants this too."

Anonymous

"I know God has forgiven me, and I've forgiven those involved, but I just can't forgive myself!" This statement has been repeated to me dozens of times by people who are working through past sin in their lives. Then follows the question *"Is* there a way to forgive myself?" The answer is yes. Let's look at what is involved in forgiving yourself.

What does it mean to forgive oneself?

Forgiving yourself means that you accept your past sin (for example, your abortion) as over and done with—finished. A part of your past, a terrible part of your past, but a part of your *past*. Forgiving yourself means you refuse to dwell on your past sinful act of abortion. As discussed in an earlier chapter, this does not mean you forget what you have done. You will never forget, in the sense of losing all memory, what you did. But you can *learn* to say with the apostle Paul, ". . . but one thing I do: forgetting what lies behind and reaching forward to what lies ahead, I press on toward the goal for the prize of the upward call of God in Christ Jesus" (Philippians 3:13–14). That doesn't mean you talk about your abortion casually or flippantly. An abortion is a serious offense against God's law. However, you are now free to discuss your abortion when opportunities arise in order to help others. None of us are proud of what we did. But we must learn to let go and go on. If God can forgive you, and He can, He can give you the strength and ability to forgive yourself.

It is interesting to note that the act of forgiving oneself is *not* mentioned in the Bible. We are instructed to forgive others and to seek forgiveness from others. Never are we told to forgive ourselves. Psalms 51:12 records David crying out for restoration: "Restore to me the joy of Thy salvation, And sustain me with a willing spirit." In speaking of forgiving ourselves, we are talking about regaining the joy of our salvation. That can happen only when all is right between you and God and between you and your fellow human beings. Think of that special moment when you first trusted Christ for salvation. That initial satisfaction of knowing all was right is what we want to regain. It is impossible for us to forgive ourselves when we still harbor ill feelings toward others. Only by relinquishing our bitterness and anger will we be totally free.

Why am I having such a hard time forgiving myself?

Perhaps this question submitted on my survey more accurately phrases the above question: "What right have I to peace and happiness when a child was killed to achieve these goals?" Paulette Hawkins wrote:

The hardest thing for me to do after my abortion was to forgive myself. I felt that I deserved to be punished. I would ask God to forgive me, but then I wouldn't accept His forgiveness. Mentally I was beating myself to death. I had been praying for God to take me, to let me die because I couldn't stand living anymore. Since I killed my baby, why should I live? I told God if He didn't let me die, then I would do something about it myself. That's when my husband had me hospitalized. He didn't even know about my abortion at that time. He just knew that for some reason I deeply hated myself.

One woman who has never had an abortion, but only contemplated one, asked, "Is it normal to feel guilty for so many years having only contemplated abortion at one time?" The very act of considering abortion has left this woman feeling guilty. Yes, it is normal to feel guilty over something we have thought or done which is wrong. What is not normal is to continue to carry the guilt once we have asked God to wash it away.

Sometimes our actions have caused irreparable damage. The baby is gone. People have been hurt. You must understand that what is done is past. You can't undo it. You can only accept God's forgiveness and go on.

I think we sometimes try to hang on to our sins. We feel we must in some way "pay" for our abortion. We looked at this in Chapter 13, which deals with punishment. If God has forgiven you (and He *has* if you have asked Him), you have begun a new life in Him (2 Corinthians 5:17). It is not within your "rights" to punish yourself for a forgiven act.

What is necessary now is to thank God for freeing you. The Bible tells you, "If therefore the Son [Jesus] shall make you free, you shall be free indeed" (John 8:36). The weight of your abortion is gone. Think of the freedom God has given you. "Blessed is he whose transgressions are forgiven, whose sins are covered. Blessed is the man whose sin the Lord does not count against him and in whose spirit is no deceit" (Psalms 32:1–2 NIV). Rejoice! Your sins are covered by the precious blood of Christ—completely and forever.

How do I justify having done something so horrible?

To justify means to make something right. You can't justify your abortion. There is nothing you can do to make it right. Only God through Jesus Christ can make it right.

How can I expect God to forgive me when I can't even forgive myself?

God's forgiveness is not contingent upon your feelings. God has forgiven *all* people. Some choose not to accept His forgiveness. Receiving God's forgiveness is contingent only upon your trusting in Christ's death, burial, and resurrection as sufficient to pay the penalty for your sins.

How can I get over feeling like a bad person instead of feeling as though I've done something bad?

This is a good question. The answer lies in understanding that God views people separately from the things they do. Did you know that God loves people who do bad things? Why? Because no one does good! Does this surprise you? Read these words from Romans 3:12: "There is none who does good, there is not even one" (see also Psalms 14:1–3; 53:1–4). Then God tells us some great news in Romans 5:8: "But God demonstrates His own love towards us, in that while we were yet sinners, Christ died for us." I'm so glad God loves us even though we do bad things (sin).

Romans 3:25 says that we are "justified [accepted by God] freely by His grace through the redemption that is in Christ Jesus." Therefore, once you trust Christ as your Savior, you are a good person (through Christ) who still sometimes does bad things.

Do I truly understand and accept God's forgiveness if I can't forgive myself?

First of all, there is no such word as "can't" in God's language. We may choose *not* to do something, but the fact is we could do it if we wanted. When you say you "can't" forgive yourself, what you really mean is you "won't" forgive yourself.

This is how I described failure to forgive yourself in *Abortion's Second Victim:*

In ancient times when a person was cast into prison, a list of his or her debts was recorded. When the debts were satisfied, the words "It is finished" were written across the list of debts. Now think of Christ as the One upon whom all your debts (sins) were written. Your debts were nailed to the cross in the form of Jesus Christ. When Christ, in His final words, cried out, "It is finished," He was canceling your debt by paying the price for you (John 19:30). If you have trusted Christ as your personal Savior, you now possess a receipt marked "It is finished." It's your proof that the reason for your guilt is gone. The debt has been paid.

Each time you permit yourself to feel guilty about your abortion, it is as if you were running to the cross to pound one more nail into Christ's body. You are saying to God, "I don't believe this one debt is paid." You are not trusting Christ's death as sufficient for paying *all* your sin—as though it were too big for Him to handle alone. If you belong to Christ, the debt *is* paid, and the reason for your guilt is gone.[1]

If you have not forgiven yourself, you may *understand* God's forgiveness and yet have failed to apply it to your own life. We must *accept* God's forgiveness in order to forgive ourselves. God willingly forgives *all* our sins at the moment of salvation when we trust Christ as our personal Savior. Forgiveness is like salvation—God extends it to us, but we don't benefit from it until we begin to appropriate it into our lives. We must learn to live what we know to be true.

If God has forgiven me, why do I still feel guilty?

The key word here is "feel." If you have truly repented of your sins, including your sin of abortion, then you are no longer guilty. The Bible tells us in Romans 8:1, "There is therefore now no condemnation for those who are in Christ Jesus." Satan would have us live defeated lives. He lost us to heaven when we trusted Christ as our personal Savior, but he wants us to be miserable as long as we live on this earth.

Peter Wilkes says, "Guilt feelings that stem from things we have done can only be removed when our actions themselves are dealt with. Dealing with the feelings alone never works because guilt is not just a feeling. We are guilty because we have done wrong. That wrongness is not a feeling—it's a fact."[2] Second Corinthians 7:10 tells us godly sorrow leads to true repentance. God uses guilt to drive us toward Him in utter helplessness because only Jesus can deal with our guilt.

If you still feel guilty, there may be a valid reason. Ask yourself two questions. Are you truly a child of God, having

1. Pam Koerbel, *Abortion's Second Victim* (Victor Books, Wheaton, Illinois, 1986), p. 146.
2. Peter Wilkes, *Overcoming Anger and Other Dragons of the Soul* (InterVarsity Press. Downers Grove, Illinois, 1987), p. 18.

come to Him through the shed blood of Christ alone for forgiveness? If so, are there any unresolved conflicts regarding your abortion which are bringing guilt? Once you settle the account, so to speak, the guilt will be gone.

In her pamphlet entitled . . . *But I Can't Forgive Myself!* Melody Green advises us to ask ourselves if we are being convicted (by the Holy Spirit) or condemned (by Satan). She correctly states that conviction is specific. Your thoughts say, "You have just lied." On the other hand, condemnation is nebulous. Thoughts such as "You aren't any good" or "God could never forgive an abortion" fill your mind. If you aren't certain which it is, ask God to clarify the situation ("God, what are you trying to tell me?"). Melody Green adds, "If it's the Lord, and if you are open to being corrected, guaranteed He will tell you."[3]

Linda Cochrane comments, "Once forgiven there is no need to find ways to punish yourself or continue to feel guilty. God wants you to feel His forgiveness. Satan would love it if God's children were rendered powerless, crippled under the emotion of guilt and feeling unworthy of forgiveness."[4] Mary Ann tells how she handles Satan's attacks: "When Satan tries to tell me that the sin of abortion is too terrible to be forgiven or brought out into the open (and the scoundrel still tries at times to induce me to believe that), I rebuke him [in the name of Jesus] and refuse to believe that lie. I am washed clean by the blood of Jesus. Praise Him forever!"

If you have trusted in the shed blood of Christ to forgive your sins, the fact is that God has forgiven you. You are no longer guilty. Live according to the facts, not according to your sometimes inaccurate feelings.

3. Melody Green, . . . *But I Can't Forgive Myself!* (Last Days Ministries, Lindale, Texas, 1985), pamphlet.
4. Linda Cochrane, *Women in Ramah: A Post Abortion Bible Study* (PACE, Falls Church, Virginia, 1986), p. 50.

Is there anything else that will help me?

The Bible says you were once alienated from God in your mind by wicked works. God has reconciled you and now holds you holy, unblamable, and irreproachable if you *continue* in hope and practice of what you *know* to be true (Colossians 1:21–23). A beautiful portion of Scripture is Colossians 2:8–15. Here we are warned to focus our beliefs and actions on Christ rather than on man because "in Him all the fulness of Deity dwells in bodily form." The passage continues to tell us that although we were dead in our sins, "He [Christ] made you alive together with Him, having forgiven us all our transgressions, having canceled out the certificate of debt. . . . He has taken it out of the way, having nailed it to the cross." Hallelujah! We are free!

Many women have written expressing their personal thoughts regarding forgiving themselves. Here are some of their words:

One of the hardest things in my past was forgiving myself. It was a day to day sometimes minute to minute decision to give it to the Lord. As I soaked myself in the Lord's forgiveness, I finally have reached the point of forgiving myself. Satan would still like to put condemnation upon me, but I reject it in the name of Jesus Christ. (Anonymous)

One person that I spoke with about this said: "If you have been able to ask God to forgive you and have accepted His forgiveness then why can't you forgive yourself? Are you more righteous than He? If He being holy and without sin can offer forgiveness then we who are with sin should be able to forgive." It sounded harsh at the time, but as it sunk in it really made sense and I think she is right. (Phyllis Lefort)

Thanks to WEBA (Women Exploited by Abortion) I received the help I needed to straighten this one out. If I repented (would never have another abortion) and was truly sorry for the sin I committed by abortion, then God forgives me. Therefore, I have no right to not forgive myself. A simple but profound truth, which I needed to hear a couple of times before I could understand and accept it. (Regina)

For a while I had to worry about my abortion, but God has made me "careless" about it. He said to cast all your cares on Him for He cares for you. I have finally been able to stop proving to God that I won't ever abort another one of His precious children. He knew it all the time, but now I know it too. After all this time I finally don't care any more because I know God loves me! I don't have to hang my head in shame anymore, because He forgave me! (Debra)

The following words of Debbie K. Weiser sum up simply and completely what your attitude should be. Write them down, think about them, and live them out day by day. "I feel so sorry for what I did but God has forgiven me and I have forgiven myself."

CHAPTER SEVENTEEN

Should I Tell Others About My Abortion?

"I'm still trying to decide how 'open' to be. I've been very 'discreet' in revealing my past . . . which I think is wise. But a part of me just wants to let it out! It is such a big part of me and affects what I do, and my reasoning. I'm struggling with the balance."

Lisa M. Bertuzzi

In Chapter Five we discussed the benefit of talking to someone about your abortion in order to work through it in your own mind. In this chapter we look into the advisability of telling others to inform them of your abortion.

Why am I afraid to speak out?

For many years my abortion was a secret shared with my husband and no one else. When the topic came up in conversation, I cried inside and sometimes outwardly too. I wanted to tell, and yet I wanted to keep it a secret. I wanted others to know how painful abortion is, both physically and emotionally. Most of all I needed to know I was accepted in spite of what I had done. Yet I knew that the more people I confided in, the greater chance there was of my secret slipping out.

Robin Fornengo puts it this way: "I still don't feel the freedom that I would like to have about sharing my abortion. There's still fear in having people find out. I'm not real open about it. . . . But I want to be able to speak out more without that fear."

Once we begin to admit to others the fact that we had an abortion, we open ourselves to ridicule and rejection. That's scary. We may fear that revealing our abortion will hurt others who, until this point, have been spared the knowledge.

Should I care what others think?

Yes, you should care what others think. It matters how people perceive you. Your testimony—that is, the way you live your life—speaks volumes. It is said that Christians are the only Bible most people will ever read. The Bible is filled with incidents of people caught in sinful situations. What they are remembered for is how they dealt with their sin and how they lived their lives from that point forward. Your changed life should speak louder than any words you may utter.

You should also care what others think when you ask them to keep your secret. Over the years, I've been privileged to help many women to resolve their abortion aftermath. Most have gone on to realize that telling others is good. However, one aborted woman, a close friend of mine, has asked me not to reveal that she once had an abortion. She is afraid of what others will think. There have been times when I've had to ask God to put a guard on my tongue so her secret will not slip out. You see, I now have the burden of bearing her secret. In some ways I wish she had not told me about her abortion, because it puts a strain on me to keep her secret.

We must learn that life is filled with people who will reject us for one reason or another—if not for our abortion, then for the way we dress or the church we attend. We can't live our lives to gain acceptance from others. We must live our lives to glorify and please Jesus Christ. Laura has a good comment: "I have to trust the Lord with how people perceive me if I share what happened to me. Before I kept it inside for fear of rejection and because of my shame. That was Satan's lie—everyone I have ever shared it with has had compassion, and felt sorry I endured such pain."

Why should I tell others?

There are several reasons why I recommend that you tell others about your abortion. The most obvious one is that if you are writing or speaking publicly, people you have not told will eventually find out. Telling those special people in your life about your abortion says to them, "I care enough about you to let you hear this from my own mouth." It's a courtesy that others will appreciate.

Prior to the release of my first book, *Abortion's Second Victim,* Leigh and I decided to tell his parents. Because Leigh was not the father of my aborted baby, there had never been a need to tell them of my abortion. Now, with the name of Koerbel to appear on the cover of a book about abortion, we felt they should be told. Again, we wanted the truth to come from our lips rather than from a friend who might chance to comment, "I saw a book the other day about abortion. Is the Koerbel who wrote it related to you?"

We sat my in-laws down at a quiet moment and told them simply and plainly that I was writing a book about something that had happened in my past. I had had an abortion and was writing to help others resolve the emotional problems that follow. Telling was our way to show love and courtesy to Leigh's parents.

Telling people about your abortion also opens the door for you to help others. You will undoubtedly run across other

149

aborted women. Some may be women who have been your friends or acquaintances for years. You may find the opportunity to join or start a support group in your community. *Nothing* has happened in our lives that is so shameful we cannot speak of it if our telling will help another person.

A primary reason to tell others about your abortion is the more people that know, the less burden you carry. Where there is no secret, there is no shame or fear of others finding out. There is a release in telling others. Read Julie's words:

Immediately after leaving the clinic I put on a front. My roommate had driven me and paid the money for me. We got home at noon. All of my roommates were there. . . . I wanted to be brave for them and not show how bad I was hurting. I managed to do that for about eight hours, when I went in my room and began to read a pro-life book I had bought. It was a harsh book and I cried hard for a couple of hours, when my roommates finally came into my room, talked with me for a long time and finally forced me to go out. I saw [the father of my baby] that night and many nights following that. Anger really began to build in me, to the point of wanting revenge— wanting someone else to feel as guilty as I did. I was very bitter towards him and men in general. . . . For weeks I lived with this guilt and shame. I'm surprised my eyes didn't fall out of my head, I cried so much! I began to keep it all inside because I felt my friends who knew were sick of hearing me. . . . That was untrue of course, but that was how I felt. Finally after a period of time of bottling it all up inside of me, I broke. Maybe I was finally tired of living the lie. Because that's what my life was—one big lie!

So I told many of my friends I had previously sworn would never know. . . . This was a great help to me. I needed to talk and I needed to stop living the lie. And my friends were wonderful and not condoning what I had done, but supporting anyway. God gave me wonderful friends who He worked through to help me. I never saw a counselor. I didn't need to, because I had about ten of them right at my side whenever I needed them—two of them Christians who were the most helpful! But that wasn't enough. I had already asked God's forgiveness, but I couldn't feel it yet. Telling my friends helped, but I was still living the lie to my family, the people most important in my life. Now the thought of telling my parents and one of my sisters still scared me beyond belief. . . . I had one sister I felt I could tell first of all. She lives [close by] and one afternoon I broke down and told her the whole story . . . from beginning to end! She is a strong Christian and I was *very* scared to tell her. But again, not condoning what I had done, she was very supportive and understanding. . . . Talking with my sister was the key. I finally *felt* forgiveness. I finally had some hope to go on.

Mary Ann gives another reason why we should tell others about our abortion:

The amazing thing that has come out of being honest with [my husband] is that he is the one who is most responsible for my being healed of the guilt and grief I experienced years after when the reality of my abortion hit me. How many times I cried on his shoulder, little by little easing out my grief and horror at what I had done! Recently, he told me it was hard for him when I suffered during those times because of his own painful feelings concerning the affair [I had had], but I guess it must have helped him to come to terms with it, too. But his feeling of compassion towards me at those times always gave him a willing ear and a tender heart. I thank God for a husband that has loved me through everything.

If someone doesn't know you hurt, they can't help you. Finally, sometimes you need to tell others in order to set things right. Debra writes, "God has been very gentle in His dealings with my past hurts and I know He has forgiven me. Hurray for the cleansing blood of Jesus! He seemed to deal with my hurt in stages—I guess I could only handle so much at a time. One of the stages I was in was the 'tell it all' stage. I told everyone in my church about the abortion and a few of my relatives. I think the stage I am moving into now is asking my parents' forgiveness. God is definitely going to have to help me through this one."

You will never experience freedom from the emotional aftermath related to your abortion as long as you refuse to tell someone you feel led to tell. Have you ever wondered why you are even considering telling that person? It may be that the Holy Spirit is prompting you to set things right.

Whom should I tell?

Every situation is different. Only you know if you can live at peace with yourself while keeping secret your abortion from someone close to you. Most women can't. They live in fear that one day that one person will find out.

As you decide whether to tell people about your abortion, many questions may arise, such as:

- Will a man love and respect me after finding out about my past experiences?
- I have only confessed my sin to three other people (besides my husband), and I really don't feel like telling just anyone. Is that considered deceptive?
- Will I ever be able to discuss the subject of abortion with complete freedom?
- I always hesitate; I feel some guilt or condemnation, and I wonder what others think of me. Why does it still hurt?
- Should I ever tell my parents? I had my abortion two years after my sister had become pregnant, carried the baby to term, and gave it up for adoption.

152

- Should I tell my parents I had an abortion? I was not under their roof at the time; I was on my own. I didn't want to hurt them back when it happened, and I don't want to hurt them now either.
- Should I tell my other children (either ones born before or after)?
- Should I share this pain with the father of that child? With my family?
- Why do I find it hard to talk to my female friends about it —especially the ones with children?
- Will my friends reject me if they know?

Now let's look at some specific people you may want to tell. Included here are some practical answers as well as some questions for you to think about.

Should I tell my boyfriend or fiancé?

One woman asked, "Should I share this with my future mate?" She answered her own question with another: "How could I not?" Only you can decide whether or not to tell your fiancé or boyfriend about your abortion. You might ask yourself, "Do I want to marry a man who refuses to forgive me a wrong of which I have repented?" Love implies forgiveness and reconciliation. A man who truly loves you should put you first, not your past sin. If he can't, it may be that he struggles with a secret sin of his own. If he is the father of your aborted baby, he may have his own guilt and grief to work through.

Linda counsels, "The only advice I have for others is 'tell him.' His reaction will tell you a lot about the person. Tell him before you marry. You never know what may happen to bring the past into the present (like my miscarriage did for me). So much better to start out with no secrets. If he cannot deal with it, then there will probably be other problems too."

Should I tell my husband?

Communication is the key to any relationship. Without it you are doomed from the start. Leigh knew about my abortion prior to us dating. Leigh is my best friend, my confidant, my lover. I would not withhold any fact regarding my past from him. That doesn't mean I just spout off an important fact without thinking (well, sometimes I do!). I try to wait until we are both calm and rested. After many years of marriage, there is not much we don't know about each other. I'm glad, because it gives each of us insight into the other's thinking and actions.

Judy Schmid gives a very practical reason for not keeping your abortion a secret from your husband:

> I didn't want to lie on my medical records so I recorded the abortion in case of complications. We [my husband and I] were at our first pre-natal check-up. . . . I had just had an internal exam and was sitting in the doctor's office. The doctor told the nurse to go get [my husband]. I heard her footsteps go down the hall and I was just about to tell the doctor not to mention my abortion when I heard [my husband's] voice. The next thing I knew, I heard the doctor say, "So, this is your second pregnancy?"
>
> I remember [my husband] staring at me with complete disbelief on his face. I couldn't look at him and I couldn't bear the thoughts that must have been going through his mind. . . . [My husband] was so hurt, not because of the abortion, but because he felt I didn't trust him or love him enough to tell him the truth. It could have been a disastrous point in our marriage and it was tense for a time. But because of [my husband's] deep love for me and our commitment to each other, we came through it!

Wouldn't you rather have your husband find out about your abortion from you? When you consider how he might feel if someone else told him, telling him yourself may not seem so difficult. The real issue here is not *should* you tell your husband, but *how* you should tell him.

Should I tell my parents?

If you are still living at home, you may find it burdensome to keep your secret from your parents. Although knowing may deeply wound them, it will give you the opportunity to talk it out, perhaps to resolve some of the conflicts that prompted you to choose abortion in the first place.

If you live independently, Patricia L. Tompkins' words may help you:

> I never believed it would be possible to tell my parents about my abortions, but the Lord worked on my heart through the reading of *Abortion's Second Victim* and the help of a close friend. One day I called my friend and my pastor [and asked them] to pray for my parents, and I went because I knew I had to confess my sins to them and ask for their forgiveness.
>
> I will not say this was easy, for this was the very hardest part of my journey. My parents had always given me the love described in 1 Corinthians 13. They always hoped, always believed, always looked for the best in me. Yes, they still demonstrate this special love to me. Because I went to them I am now free from the worry of them finding out through someone else. I am fully free to help others who suffer from the after effects of abortion through the Lord's grace in my own life.

Linda has decided not to tell her parents. She gives these reasons: "I've never told my parents. My mother and I are still not close and she would not understand all I've been through. On the other hand I believe it would hurt my dad that I never was able to confide in him. I realize now that he would have stood by me back then. But now I feel it's best he not know." Each woman must decide whether to tell her parents. I do see from Linda's comments that she has prejudged her parents' reaction. They may respond entirely differently than she thinks. You'll never know the understanding and compassion your parents may give you until you tell them about your abortion.

Should I tell my children?

A woman writes, "My children are three and one. I have been publicly speaking about my abortions to local churches to inform the community of what is going on. I know one day I will have to tell them. I don't want them to find out from someone else." I think this woman has hit the nail on the head. If there is any chance of your children finding out about your abortion (and children are more perceptive than we realize), better it comes from your own lips than from anyone else's.

If you are not writing or speaking publicly, you may decide to wait until they are teenagers or adults. One woman felt she would tell them if "they run into a situation where it would help." My only thought here is that by telling them about your abortion before a crisis situation (possibly pregnancy) develops in their own life, you may impress upon your children the painful consequences of sex prior to marriage.

Another woman shares, "I am trusting that the Lord will prepare my children if He wants me to share the pain of my abortion with them and He will cover it with His grace. He will let me know when and if they are ready and/or need to know."

Even if you decide not to tell your children about your abortion, please speak to each one and tell them that although you hope they will never get "in trouble," if they do, they can come to you for help. Many girls and women tell me

156

that if they had felt able to bring their "problem" to their parents, the abortion would never have taken place.

Should I tell my friends?

Stephanie shares her thoughts: "I am so scared of losing some close friendships if they ever found out that I had an abortion. As such good friends, I kind of feel like I need to tell them, and that I should just accept the consequences, but I love them so much, I don't want them to hate me."

Making yourself vulnerable comes with the trust that develops with close friends. I think you will experience relief once you get your abortion out in the open with women close to you. One woman states, "Having other women to share with heals in itself. I think the more you try to hide it the worse it becomes. Just like Psalm 52 says, it starts eating away at you."

How widely should I share my secret?

Once I married and moved to a new location where people did not know about my past, my personal policy was to tell people on a "need to know" basis. The number of people I told depended upon the circumstances. Initially, only my husband knew. I also told a psychiatrist. Eventually I told my pastor because I felt I needed counsel. One friend knew. My secret was well kept and burning inside of me for many years.

Prior to my first book, I wrote an article which was published in *Moody Monthly* magazine. At the publisher's request, and to my relief, it was printed anonymously. Circumstances prompted me to tell a few other people when the article came out. One woman I remember in particular had placed me on a pedestal. She was a new Christian and thought I, a "mature" believer, could do no wrong. One day I handed her a copy of my article and said, "Would you read this and give me your opinion?" This friend had gotten pregnant out of wedlock, married the father, and had her baby. I respected her for her strong decision. After reading the article, she said it was sad and she didn't understand how anyone could do that. I looked her right in the eye and said, "I wrote that article. I had an abortion. I am telling you because you need to know that all people have sin in their life. Just because they are Christians doesn't mean they led a perfect life before or after their conversion."

As I began writing *Abortion's Second Victim*, I desired prayer support and also to locate other aborted women. I sent a letter to all the seminarians (Leigh was in his final year at Capital Bible Seminary) seeking their help. Now everyone in our immediate circle of friends knew about me. I can tell you, it was fairly easy to write the letter, but much tougher to face people in person knowing they knew what I had done. As publication time neared, Leigh and I discussed and prayed about putting my real name on the book. We decided that since God had forgiven me I had no reason to feel guilty about the contents of the book. If someone could be helped, then so be it. We included my name and address in the introduction, knowing that some women had no one to talk to about their abortions. Letters and phone calls began to reach me as women found an outlet for expressing their pain. I have each letter, and I treasure them as proof of God's love and honor of my commitment to respond honestly to a sensitive and personal issue.

How widely should you share your secret? Remember this —as long as there is at least one person from whom you try to hide your abortion, you will always live in fear of that person finding out. When you are hiding something, that thing has the power to destroy you. The walls of shame and fear you have built around yourself will crumble and fall once you disclose your secret. This doesn't mean you must publicly proclaim the fact that you had an abortion. But you should seriously consider telling those people whose names keep popping into your mind regarding your abortion.

What if I've already told someone, but wish I hadn't?

Diane writes, "My stumbling block now is that I regret having told my mother about the abortion. Before I was healed I went to a psychiatrist and they said I should think about telling my mother my secret. She never knew a thing—that's how easy it was! One morning last winter when I was deeply depressed I called her and crying a lot I told her. I then felt relieved awhile but now regret it and wish she never knew about it. She said she wouldn't tell anyone else but we don't even talk about it."

You cannot undo the fact that you told your mother about your abortion. I don't know all the facts surrounding it, but I assume your mother loves you and is concerned for you. However, it must have come as a shock to her, and she may find it difficult to discuss. Remember, her grandchild was aborted. Is your mother a Christian? If not, discussing your abortion and the forgiveness you have found through Jesus would be a good testimony to her. In any event, I believe you would do well to ask your mother's forgiveness for any hurt you have caused her. Pray about speaking to her again and do it when the time is right.

What will others think of me?

Now we're down to the bottom line. Our pride rises up to defend our position of remaining silent. Will our silence change the opinions of those around us? Or is our prideful silence merely hindering our healing process?

Some people may look at an aborted woman and think, "She made her choice—now she's paying for it." I remember back to 1970. New York State had passed a law that legalized abortion-on-demand through the twenty-fourth week of pregnancy. My parents and I discussed the cruelty, the monstrousness of a woman killing her own child for convenience. The thought was abhorrent to me. An acquaintance at college had secretly flown to another country the previous year for a weekend. It was generally understood she had had an abortion. She looked so drained when she returned, and during the months following, all the gaiety and spontaneity left her. Yet I secretly condemned her for her actions—she was a baby killer. . . .

Sometimes it's easy to condemn—to think "That could never happen to me." How differently I view things since my own abortion.

A more likely situation is that you were present when people were discussing abortion. Someone may have made a comment similar to this: "What kind of a monster could kill her own baby?" Those words cut to the quick, don't they? Most people do not realize that whenever abortion is discussed, at least one aborted women is usually present. Such people don't mean to hurt you. It simply never occurred to them someone within hearing distance had actually experienced an abortion. I have found that although people often say unfeeling words when speaking of abortion in general, they usually sympathize when they personally know an aborted woman.

Mary Ann wrote, quoting from *Abortion's Second Victim,* "You said, '[God] may ask you to go where you are most afraid because He wants to show you that He alone can see you through your fears.' Also, by hiding my sin from the body of Christ, the church of believers, I am missing out on experiencing their acceptance of me and love for me despite my great sin."

Psalms 56:11 encourages us with these words: "In God I have put my trust, I shall not be afraid. What can man do to me?"

CHAPTER EIGHTEEN

How Do I Tell Those I Love?

"In being more open and involved I must begin by being more open with my family. . . . As God has prepared me He also has prepared the hearts of those my disclosure will affect the most."

Wendy

After the decision has been reached to tell your husband, your children, or other people, the next major question becomes *"How* do I tell them? What, exactly, do I say?" We would all breathe a huge sigh of relief if we were to read, "Say these words and you are guaranteed to reach the hardest heart, soothe the hurting heart, and mend the broken heart." Unfortunately, there is no formula that works every time. You are a unique individual, and your abortion experience has aspects that personalize it and make it different from all other abortion experiences, including other abortions you may have had. Add to this the unique personality and background of the person you plan to tell, and it becomes clear why "pat" answers are neither available nor workable.

Are there any general guidelines I can follow?

Careful planning on your part will serve you well as you prepare to share the depths of your heart with another person. Following are some guidelines that should prove helpful to you:

- Prayerfully select an opportune time (e.g., NOT when your husband is exhausted from a long, hard day at work).
- Ask God to give you the right words to touch the person you wish to tell.
- Pray before you speak that God will soften the heart of the person you tell to receive your abortion with understanding and compassion.
- Keep it simple (especially with young children).
- Pick a time when you will not be interrupted (e.g., phone off hook, dog outside, children napping or with sitter).
- Speak sincerely, quietly, and calmly.
- If your children are unfamiliar with terms such as sin, repentance, and forgiveness, take some time *before* you speak of your abortion to explain the terms.

What reactions can I expect?

Try to prepare yourself for possible reactions, which may include unbelief, shock, understanding, misunderstanding, coldness, compassion, rejection, or acceptance.

A person's initial reactions may or may not reveal his or her deepest feelings about your abortion. Have you ever reacted with shock to some startling news, only to calm down a few minutes later to deal sensibly and caringly about what happened? Remember, the person you are telling probably

162

has no idea you have had an abortion. It will be the furthest thing from his or her mind when you say you need to talk about something important. A million different thoughts may race through his or her mind, and then you zing him or her with "I had an abortion." Don't let the initial reaction daunt you. Give it time to sink in.

To give a few examples: My parents were shocked but compassionate. My boyfriend was stunned, scared, and suspicious. All my friends on campus knew about my abortion thanks to a juicy secret that someone failed to keep; some were shocked, others awed, and some never spoke to me again. My psychiatrist passed it off as of no importance to my current problem (my abortion *was* my current problem). The first friend I told was calm and understanding (she had problems in her life too!). The next friend I told was compassionate but amazed at what I told her (after all, I *was* a pastor's wife). A pastor friend betrayed no emotion (but he's trained to react that way).

A woman who was married at the time she aborted says, "I also found that people are shocked to think that *I* had an abortion, especially being married. Sometimes I feel they look at me differently. Other times, I think they wonder why I don't seem remorseful. But God has helped me deal with it completely."

When we tell any given person, even someone close such as a mother or husband, about our abortion, we present him or her with a subject that may tear open his or her own background. We can never know everything about a person, no matter how close we become. Events in people's past contribute to their current thinking and reactions. A mother may have had an abortion, lost a child to miscarriage or illness, or placed a child for adoption rather than abort it. Telling her may open old wounds. It may reveal the very act she dreaded happening to you. A husband may have wounds in his past which are still unhealed. Your hurt may rekindle his old hurts. If at all possible, please try to talk it out. Your abortion can be the opener to a flow of communication that until now

163

was stopped by time and fear of "what someone else will think." You may be surprised that the people you tell have wanted to tell you about something equally important to them, but feared what *you* would think or say. You know, abortion is not the worst sin in the world. We think it is because it happened to us. To other people, their sin is the worst because it happened to them.

How do I tell my child about my abortion?

The most traumatic personal experience I've encountered regarding revealing my abortion was when I told my son. *Abortion's Second Victim* was about to be published and Michael was six years old. Leigh and I decided he should be told about my abortion because we wanted him to hear from my lips rather than from someone who unthinkingly might say, "So Mommy had an abortion, huh?"

Mike loves beautiful things, collections (anything from scraps of paper to magic tricks), math, and most of all his brother and sisters. As a very sensitive six-year-old, he analyzed life's events with the wisdom of a sixty-year-old. Now I was about to tell him a truth that would shatter most adults. It would influence his perception of God and life and me.

I prayerfully and carefully chose a time when Mike and I were both rested, calm, well, and alone. As we sat down together, I thought the lump in my throat would never permit words to pass. "Oh, God," I prayed, "please give me the words, the perfect words, to share with Mike my deepest feelings in a way he will understand." This is what I told Mike:

"Mike, Mommy needs to talk to you about something that happened a long time ago. It is something that happened to me before Daddy and I were married and before you were born."

"What is it, Mommy?"

This was it. Now he sat before me—earnest, inquiring,

expectant. "Oh Lord, give me wisdom!" This small boy who had accepted Christ as his personal Savior at the age of three because he wanted to spend eternity with Jesus in heaven. This boy whose first prayers were "God, please help the sick person in the ambulance" each time he heard a siren. This boy who knew only love and happiness. What would my words do to his secure world?

"You know Mommy has been writing a book, don't you? Do you know what the book is about?"

"No. Is it a good book?"

"Yes, a good book that Mommy and Daddy pray God will use to help many people who are hurting. The book is about abortion. Have you ever heard that word before?"

"No. What does it mean?"

"Abortion is when a mommy has a baby in her tummy and the baby is taken out of her tummy before it is ready to be born." Mike had a younger brother and sister at this time and understood that babies grew in a mommy's "tummy." "The baby dies because it can't live yet outside the mommy. Abortion kills a tiny baby before it is born.

"A long time ago I had a baby growing in my tummy. I did a terrible thing and had an abortion. I killed that baby. It was a sin. I have asked God to forgive me, and He has forgiven me. Now I want to ask you to forgive me for killing a baby that would have been your older brother. Will you forgive me, Michael?" By this time tears were streaming down my cheeks. Mike knew I was hurting so very much and that what I had just told him was of great importance to me.

"Yes, I forgive you, Mommy."

"You know, Michael, each of us does some bad things in our lives. Some sins do more harm than others. I can never get back the baby I killed."

Mike thought for a moment and then with a very serious expression replied, "Isn't God good, Mommy? He gave you three children to replace the one you lost!"

God spoke to me that day through my child, and His love and compassion are ever before me.

How old should my child be before I tell him?

I don't recommend telling very young children (under age six or seven) about abortion for the simple reason that they usually cannot understand. Michael was very advanced for his age and able to grasp the main concepts when presented simply. However, he is ten years old now and can barely remember our talk. Our other children are six, four, and two, and I will wait before telling them.

If you do decide to tell your children, keep it simple. If possible, go to the library beforehand and borrow a book showing pictures of an unborn baby's development. Children are naturally curious. Seeing a picture of what an unborn baby looks like will help them understand it was a baby you aborted.

Tell them the truth, stressing that you know you were wrong and that God has forgiven you. With an older child, it might prove a good object lesson to mention that although God forgives, there is usually a penalty to pay with any sin. In this case, you live with the memory of having killed your own child.

How do I tell my fiancé or boyfriend about my abortion?

A lady named Pat says:

> I had two abortions ten years ago. The second abortion came only two months after I had received Jesus as my Savior. It seemed as though I had broken God's heart *forever* and I certainly wondered if any other man would care for and love me. About five years later I met my husband-to-be. Since this time I had received God's forgiveness for the abortions. The Lord had told me He

would confirm when I was to tell my boyfriend. One night, after dating several months, he told me that he really loved me. I knew then that I must be honest and share my testimony. This man sat there listening very intently to my story, and he began to weep and reach out to hold me. He said that if this other person could not accept the responsibility, that he would. I knew then that this was the man God had picked for my mate (we became engaged that night) and that God was showing me His wonderful forgiveness through another special human being. Things haven't always been perfect—we still sometimes struggle with thoughts about the abortions— but it's good to know someone understands. Most of all, Jesus loves me and cares the most.

How do I tell my husband about my abortion?

Two women share how they told their husbands:

About six weeks into my therapy I decided to tell my husband about my abortion. . . . I gave him a poem to read which I wrote dealing with my abortion. I held my breath as he read it, wondering—will he still love me, will he want anything to do with me? He took me in his arms and held me as I cried and cried and cried. I didn't know it was possible to cry so hard for so long. Abortion is a death and I had never allowed myself to grieve. (Paulette Hawkins)

I had managed to stuff the memories of [my] affair and abortion deep into my subconscious until a situation forced them to the surface. I shudder to think what would have become of our marriage had the memories not been shaken to the surface. Until then I didn't think about them, ever!

After [my husband] and I had been married about six months, we ran into some friends we'd associated with at the time I [had had my affair and abortion]. All of my stuffed down memories flooded into my consciousness. I knew that this secret was TOO BIG for me to contain. Besides, [my husband] and I valued honesty in our relationship, and I felt that keeping a secret like this was somehow deceitful. Also, it might perhaps backfire on us someday. I was scared to death to tell him, but without thinking about it too much I went up to him the following Saturday and said I had to talk to him. . . . I just spit it out. I explained . . . [about the affair and] how I wished it had never happened. I could see [my husband] was approaching the point of exploding. . . . He had known the man and knew how he had used lots of girls. . . . He kicked over a potted plant, banged his fist on a car, and put his head down on the roof of the car. I saw there were tears in his eyes. He looked in a state of shock, hurt, disbelief and rage all at once. At this point I was very much afraid he wouldn't feel the same about me after this, and I hadn't even told him about the abortion yet. I forget what ensued directly after this, but I remember being in our bedroom later in the day. I told him about the abortion. I think we were both crying, but we were able to talk about it. And thanks to God, I knew he still loved me. I could see how hurt he felt over the whole thing—the affair much more than the abortion. I felt so awful and guilty. How I wished none of it had happened to mar our marriage. Afterwards, though, we both felt relieved (me, especially) for having no more secrets. We resolved to always be honest with each other. (Mary Ann)

Mary Ann also offers some practical guidelines to women who haven't yet told their husbands about a past abortion:

I would say to pray first to ask the Lord [to help] you to be honest and courageous, and to give your husband an understanding heart. . . . Then I would say to get it over with as soon as possible. Hard tasks become monstrous if we think and worry about them too much beforehand and put them off. Then, I would say to trust in your husband's love for you. Also, to trust that the Holy Spirit is present in our marriages that we may minister Jesus' love and healing to each other. I believe that when we keep secrets from each other . . . we cut ourselves off from forgiveness and healing. It will become lonely and overwhelming to keep these things hidden.

Will the person I tell forgive me?

We may need to seek forgiveness from someone. This offers a perfect opportunity to bring up your abortion. You might say, "I have done something wrong and need to ask your forgiveness." I asked forgiveness in person whenever possible because that is what the Bible teaches in Matthew 5:24–25. I asked my parents' forgiveness for murdering their first grandchild. They may not have offered all the emotional support I wanted, but they always wanted me to have my baby. I went against their wishes when I aborted. You may have to seek forgiveness from the father of your aborted baby. If you are now dating or married, this can open a wonderful world of communication to the two of you. I had to seek Leigh's forgiveness. Although he was not the father, because of my abortion I had not been the wife God had told me to be. For many years I still loved and wanted to be with the father of my aborted baby. Leigh was denied the companionship, sexual relationship, and love he deserved. Seeking Leigh's forgiveness let him understand I knew I was wrong.

Some people will not forgive you. They may even *say* they forgive you, but they secretly hold your abortion against you. They may do this from some private hurt inside of them or from a lack of understanding regarding God's forgiveness. The important fact for you to embrace is that once you have asked a person to forgive you with love and sincerity in your heart, you stand clean before God. If these people fail to forgive you, it is now *their* problem. As difficult as it may be, continue to show love and tenderness toward the person who fails to forgive you. Don't allow the other person's wrong attitude to affect your peace with God.

What if the person doesn't want to discuss my abortion?

If people already know about your abortion as a fact, but you now want to discuss it more fully, you could simply approach them with the words "Could we talk about my abortion?" or "I have a problem with something and I am hoping you can help me with it." This latter phrase places the other person in a position to offer advice and help.

Abortion is an emotionally charged topic. The very word stirs hidden feeling inside each person. Please try to speak calmly, quietly, and sincerely. Keep your voice low but audible. If the person you are telling becomes loud or enraged, keep your cool. Two of you flying off the handle will only make matters worse. The Bible wisely tells us, "A gentle answer turns away wrath, But a harsh word stirs up anger" (Proverbs 15:1). It may be necessary to postpone further discussion until another time. Seek God's wisdom before bringing up your abortion to that person again. Ask God to prepare his or her heart.

How can I keep it from hurting those I love?

One woman made the statement "I need to know how to be sensitive in my sharing." I think this is a key principle in how we tell others about our abortion experience. There is no easy way to tell someone you have had an abortion. Likewise, there is no formula of words to say. The Bible tells us to "speak the truth in love" (Ephesians 4:15). Gentleness in relating the facts of your abortion is necessary. Remember that as abortion hurt you, so it will often hurt those you choose to tell. Abortion affects the lives of all those around you. People will hurt both for you and for their own loss once it is revealed to them. Your love, gentleness, and understanding of their feelings will go far to ease their pain. Remember, just as you needed someone to "be there" to hear you, so the people you choose to tell might need you to "be there" for them with a listening and understanding heart.

CHAPTER NINETEEN

How Can I Help My Husband Deal with My Abortion?

"We have a continent of men who have shared with their mates in this decision in one way or another. And the hurt is as deep."

Wendy

An abortion affects many people. It is my personal desire that the people affected by my abortion resolve their feelings and put my abortion behind them. But the person I most want to understand and fully accept my abortion is the man with whom I share my life—my husband, Leigh.

For some of us, our husband must learn to accept our abortion as something of which he had no part. For others, abortion was an act which affected both of you intimately because your husband is the father of the baby you aborted. In either instance your husband may or may not have known about your abortion prior to your marriage. Yet in both cases, our men live intimately with a woman who is in the daily process of learning to accept the fact that she killed her unborn baby. Our husbands must cope not only with our pain but also with their own innermost feelings regarding this act.

My husband is the father of my aborted baby. How can I help him to grieve?

Just as it was necessary for you to grieve, so your husband must grieve for the baby he lost. Remember, his methods of grieving may differ from yours. He may not grieve as intensely or as long. He fathered the baby biologically. However, a man can never share the intimacy of carrying a child within his body. Therefore, the reality of it being a baby, *his* baby, that you killed may not come readily to him.

Talk to your husband about your feelings. Tell him what it was like carrying a baby in your womb. Tell him why you know it was a baby rather than just a blob of tissue. Show him pictures of an unborn baby's development. Share ways you found to grieve. Encourage him to forgive people involved in your abortion. Be sensitive to his needs. Try to help him open up, but don't force the issue. Touch each other physically and emotionally. Cry together. Pray together. If your husband is not a Christian, share your faith in Christ and tell how He has helped you.

Second Corinthians 1:3–4 encourages us with these words: "Praise be to the God and Father of our Lord Jesus Christ, the Father of compassion and the God of all comfort, who comforts us in all our troubles, so that we can comfort those in any trouble with the comfort we ourselves have received from God" (NIV).

My husband (not the baby's father) seems ambivalent toward my abortion. Doesn't he care?

If you still carry guilt about your abortion, you may believe your husband should feel guilty too. Yet your abortion is part

173

of his life only because it is part of yours. Your husband can't know your innermost feelings until you share them with him.

Following are my husband's thoughts from several years ago:

> The abortion only affected me indirectly since it was not my child and I was only related to the situation after the fact. The only effect was concerning my wife's reaction to it. However, at the time I was still somewhat indifferent towards the idea of abortion. It affected our relationship when she was unable to come to grips with the guilt and ill feelings that began to emerge. She began having nightmares and any discussion of the subject was strained and extremely difficult. Even being in a room where the topic was being discussed was unbearable for my wife.

Part of Leigh's indifference was due to the fact that he didn't know how to deal with *me*. That caused him to retreat from discussing my abortion in order to avoid agitating me.

One wife writes, "My husband (not the aborted baby's father) won't open up with me, or is unable to share any emotion in this. I only told him about it last year, after nine years of marriage. He was very sweet and understanding that 'we all make mistakes,' but that's as much as he's cared to discuss it." Whatever you do, don't belittle, berate, or badger your husband. Give him time to adjust to your abortion. It is possible your husband truly accepts your abortion as part of your past. Be thankful. Many women struggle with husbands who refuse to let their wives forget about their past sins.

Can my new husband ever really know the depth of my pain, the scarring that lives in my heart, and the emotional aftermath?

No person other than you can ever fully comprehend what you have endured because of your abortion. But your husband can come to respect your feelings if you take time to explain them. Linda writes, "I'm not sure he understands the pain it still sometimes brings, but he is supportive and that is more than I prayed for."

Why doesn't my husband (it was his baby) grieve as I do?

Each person grieves differently. Men in our culture have been conditioned to keep their emotions in check. It's important that you don't force your husband to "feel" as you do. It would be wrong for him to pretend to grieve just to satisfy you. Remember, for some people, grieving takes longer to begin. Also keep in mind that although your husband may not grieve *as* you do, he may grieve as *intensely* as you.

Phyllis Lefort explains:

We never talked about the abortion with each other or to anyone. Both of us avoided the subject as much as we could—excusing ourselves from conversations, turning off TV or radio programs, reading nothing but titles. Twelve years we kept it secret. One day while having tea with two Christian friends the subject of abortion came up. I got up and went to another room and wept. I couldn't handle the silence any longer. Slowly I began to tell these two friends the whole story. A while later I talked with [my husband]. I was amazed to find out that he was carrying around a lot of guilt and the same

175

feelings I have had he also had. [My husband], unlike most men, is very open and shares his feelings and thoughts even more than I do. . . . Each time deeper feelings came out and more details came out and slowly, step-by-step [we were] being healed.

Your husband may have wanted the baby you aborted. He may resent the fact he had no legal recourse.[1] Then, too, at the time of your decision, he may have felt boxed into a corner—a trade-off faced him. He may have felt he had to sacrifice the baby to meet your need or to save his relationship with you. It may be that he has grieved longer inside than you realize.

My prospective fiancé knows the situation and used to be friends with the guy. He has a hard time dealing with it. How can I help him?

The father of my aborted baby was Leigh's fraternity brother. I know it was difficult for Leigh to socialize with "Tim" (as I shall call him), to know I had slept with him, to know Tim had ignored his responsibility. Leigh had to resolve his anger and hurt just as I had done. He had to learn to forgive Tim for the wrong he had done to me and my baby, and to forgive me for my acts of fornication and abortion. As long as your husband refuses to forgive, the pain of what you went through will continue to fester inside of him.

Forgiveness is a personal and individual choice. Explain to your husband why you chose to forgive and the weight that was lifted from you because you forgave. Then let your man make his own decision.

Because of our situation at college, Leigh and I were

1. It is ironic that in America men have no legal recourse to save their unborn baby's life, and yet men are required to support the child even if they wanted him aborted and the woman chose to give birth.

constantly thrown into contact with Tim. It was especially difficult for Leigh because he knew I still had strong emotional attachments to Tim. Added to this was the fact that as the years went by, I often spoke of Tim when discussing my abortion. The advice I *want* to give is, try to avoid contact with and discussion of your aborted baby's father. I know this will not be possible in many cases. The father of your aborted baby may be a close family friend or business associate. Also, although your husband may never meet your aborted baby's father, it may be necessary for you to speak of him as you talk through your abortion aftermath. If your husband refuses to listen, respect his wishes. Do your talking to a priest or pastor or a woman friend. Although talking about events and people concerned with your abortion helps you, some men have not reached the point in their lives where they can calmly discuss their woman's relationship with another man. It takes more than maturity to handle what we are asking our men to hear. It takes supernatural understanding.

But God's grace is sufficient. One husband and wife have dealt so completely with her abortion that they are now close friends with the father of the aborted baby and his wife. This living example of Christ's power to mend hearts and restore relationships stands as encouragement to each of us that any conflict can be resolved.

How do I deal with a husband who wants to ignore his responsibility in the abortion?

Your job is to love your husband and be the godly wife God wants you to be. It is God's responsibility to "deal" with your husband regarding his part in your abortion. Pray for your husband. Submit to him. Do not be bitter toward him. God says not to let the sun go down on your wrath—in other words, resolve your feelings of anger and resentment before you go to bed.

If you believe you must "deal" with your husband's

improper response to your abortion, you will never heal and your husband will eventually resent you for your intrusion. First Peter 3:1–2 offers wise counsel: "In the same way, you wives, be submissive to your own husbands so that even if any of them are disobedient to the Word, they may be won without a word by the behavior of their wives, as they observe your chaste and respectful behavior."

Since my husband was involved, how do we move to a new, trusting relationship?

In order to move to a trusting relationship, you and your husband must seek forgiveness from God and from each other for your abortion. Then you must choose to accept the abortion as part of your past.

One aborted father told me with tears in his eyes that the responsibility for the abortion he and his wife consented to is *not* fifty-fifty. "Pam," he said, "each of us is *100 percent* responsible for our action. I only thank God He has forgiven us."

CHAPTER TWENTY

How Will My Abortion Affect My Other Children and Their Relationship to Me?

"Now because of what I've gone through emotionally (and physically) I think I will be a better mother. A very good mother."

Jill Iversen

One issue that dominates a woman's thinking concerns the affect of her abortion on her living children. The first question asked and answered lays the groundwork for the suggestions set forth in this chapter.

What is a mother?

This question brings specific perceptions to each individual's mind. I picture my own mother: gentle, loving, giving, unselfish, unintrusive, and concerned—she's, well, she's motherly! The dictionary provides the technical definition: "A woman who has borne a child; that which gives birth to something, is the origin or source of something, or nurtures in the manner of a mother."[1] *Nurture*—that's the key word in the definition. A mother is a nurturer of the children for whom she is responsible, be they biological, adoptive, or custodial. To nurture means to promote the development, training, and rearing of someone or something. Thus, a mother is someone whose job is to promote the welfare of those for whom she cares.

When I become pregnant and people say, "Is this your first pregnancy?" can I say yes?

This is a tougher question than it first appears. If you answer yes you will be lying; to answer no opens the door for embarrassing questions.

Personally, since Leigh was not my aborted baby's father, I truthfully answered, "This is our first baby." I didn't emphasize the word "our," and people never questioned my phrasing. If you are married to your aborted baby's father, you might say, "I'm so excited and nervous about my first birth experience!"

If you believe you can emotionally handle the situation, you might say, "This will be my first living baby" or "No, this is my second pregnancy." Most people will assume you had a miscarriage. If questioned, gently tell people you experienced an abortion. Don't be afraid to let people know you are real and have made a mistake in your past.

What sort of mother will I be when I do have a baby that I can hold in my arms?

Because I had not yet dealt with my abortion, it was difficult going through that next pregnancy. Well-meaning people

1. *Webster's New World Dictionary of the American Language,* college edition (The World Publishing Company, New York, 1966), p. 960.

gave advice and cautions about the pain of labor. Because I had aborted by saline injection, the baby was dead and my body had to do all the work. I had already endured the most painful vaginal delivery possible. Yet I could not admit this.

As the months ticked by, I listened in silence to discussions concerning caring for a new baby. During natural childbirth classes I felt separated from the excitement of other new mothers expecting their first baby. I wondered how I would ever face the day I would hold my own living child. How would I feel? Would I love him or her? Most of my feelings were perfectly normal apprehensions any expectant mother faces. I didn't know that back then. I thought I only felt the way I did because of my abortion.

Then I went into labor. The months of preparation culminated in an easy, natural birth with my husband at my side. When Michael was placed into my arms, I knew what being a mother meant and I cherished the gift God had given me.

Much has been written on bonding. It is true that guilt, self-hatred, low self-esteem, and depression can affect the bonding process with your unborn baby. But the problem lies within your mind because of unresolved emotional conflicts, and not with your new baby. During a pregnancy subsequent to an abortion, our tendency is to focus on the aborted baby. This is so harmful. Dr. Philip Ney comments, "It is generally recognized that an unresolved loss interferes with the process of attaching to a new child.[2] Instead, we must seek to completely resolve our abortion's aftermath. Then we will be free to consciously focus our thoughts on the new baby—the one that will be born alive and capable of loving us in return.

You will be exactly the sort of mother you set your mind to be. You can choose to concentrate on your past abortion and adversely affect both your lives, or you can choose to nurture and love your new child.

2. Dr. Philip G. Ney, "The Child and Death," *New Zealand Medical Journal,* Vol. 96, No. 726, February 23, 1983, p. 129.

Sometimes I feel that with each child I have, I grieve more for the child I aborted. Why?

It's natural to occasionally think of your aborted child. With any child who has died, a mother feels sorrow. Each new child brings back thoughts of the child you lost. If you have more than one child, you know each new *birth* brings back memories of previous births of your other children. However, if you still genuinely grieve for your aborted baby, you need to work on accepting his death.

How may my other children respond once they know I aborted their sibling?

In the years ahead you will hear of "survivor syndrome." For instance, surviving children may wonder why they weren't aborted, they may become angry and hostile, or they may fear future rejection by their parents if predetermined standards set by themselves or their parents are not met. Children must learn to settle their negative emotions regarding your abortion, just as you learned to settle yours.

Concern exists over the fact that some children playact death when they learn of a sibling's abortion. I see this as a normal response to learning about death. A child learns about weddings and playacts a wedding. A child learns about homemaking and playacts keeping house. A child learns about truck drivers and playacts driving a truck. So with death a young child examines his feelings and expands his understanding by playacting what he has learned.

I believe children usually respond to stress more straightforwardly than adults. They haven't learned to conceal their honest feelings. One mother wrote, "My youngest child said, 'I'm glad it wasn't me.' They were shocked at the news. However, they've assured me that they still love me. I'm sure at times they wonder about that brother or sister they never knew." A child's faith is simple and complete, and if properly nurtured, it will guide him safely through this experience.

How could my negative response to my abortion affect my children?

Dr. Ney delineates three potential reactions of our children to abortion:[3]

1. *The haunted child.* Abortion is mysterious to him due to lack of information. He believes something tragic has occurred, but he is terrified to find out just what because he fears the truth will be worse than what he has imagined.
2. *The bound child.* He lives a sheltered life, overprotected by parents who fear they may also lose him. The parents may remain ambivalent toward the child to insure that if something happens to him, their pain won't be as great. This child may become alienated from his parents or overly dependent upon them. The child may also abuse his parents, who in turn believe this abuse is their due punishment for the abortion.
3. *The substitute child.* This is the replacement child, expected to fulfill the dreams and hopes the parents had for the dead child. Because this baby is so wanted, our expectations may be too high. We feel cheated when the child doesn't live up to our hopes, and we take out our frustrations on the child. "Thus, it is not surprising to find that the much wanted replacement child is more frequently abused."

Dr. Ney concludes, "Surviving siblings most likely to be entrapped in one of these three syndromes have parents who: (a) have not been able to mourn a death in the family; (b)

3. Ibid., pp. 128–29.

have wished for a child's death; (c) are survivors themselves; (d) are at least partly responsible for a child's death; (e) are inhibited by personal or cultural prohibitions against discussing death; (f) have a physician who cannot or will not discuss a child's death with them."[4]

It seems clear that problems with living children can be expected if we don't resolve our abortion's aftermath. The key to avoiding problems lies with us. Once we correct our attitudes, the child will be freed to live a normal life.

How can I help my children to accept my abortion?

How you tell them makes all the difference. Hold off telling them until you have resolved your anger, bitterness, and guilt. Kids are sharp. They pick up on our vocal inflections and facial expressions more often than we may realize. You don't want to portray your abortion in a false light or transfer guilt and anger to your children. For instance, telling your children that "Mommy really got a raw deal from some people who lied to her about unborn babies" tells your children you are angry, resentful, and casting blame on someone else. They may not understand in adult vocabulary, but they understand with their emotions. How much better to approach your abortion with the words "Mommy did something wrong, and she wants you to know about it and understand why it was wrong." This tells your children you can make and have made mistakes, that you are willing to admit them, and that you have corrected them. It's an object lesson that can't be beat!

Full and clear communication is essential in any interpersonal relationship. Honesty is the best policy. Allow your child to ask questions. Dr. Ney states, "Surviving children cannot ask questions about a tragedy when their parents won't talk about their own experience of it. . . . Parents

4. Ibid., p. 129.

184

who feel guilty may try to share that guilt with surviving children. Too frequently children readily accept the blame. They realize that to carry the blame relieves their parents' distress and helps maintain family stability, but to carry the guilt severely inhibits and depresses children."[5]

Encourage discussion. Even though the discussion may be painful for you, it may be necessary for your child to talk it out. Allow the child to see your grief, tears, pain. Honestly express your sorrow over your abortion. Pray together. Let your child know he or she is loved unconditionally and individually by you. Spend time with your child. Hold and cuddle your child. Love is proven not by words but by actions.

Assure your child that abortion is not something you would ever again consider. It was wrong. You didn't know it then, but you know it now.

Consider telling your children about your abortion before they reach their teen years, especially if you mention your abortion in their presence. It is far better to tell them than let them guess whether or not you had an abortion.

We must be sensitive to our children's needs. They need not only unconditional love and affection from us, but assurance that God loves them unconditionally too. Instilling in your child an understanding of and belief in his own personal value to God, to you, and to himself is vital for helping him deal with any of life's problems.

Part of our responsibility as nurturers also includes instilling in our children an understanding of God's grace and forgiveness. Like you, your children have a resource for coping with death—the Holy Spirit, who provides comfort and peace. Young children are amazingly resilient. They easily forgive and forget because their young brains are uncluttered by years of built-up hurt and resentment.

5. Ibid., p. 128.

How might my abortion adversely affect my mothering?

If you allow it to, an abortion can seriously affect your attitude and behavior toward your living children. As a result, they can be devastatingly affected. *Any* mother can become overprotective,[6] ambivalent, or abusive. Abuse can be physical or emotional.

The perfect mother does not exist. No matter how hard we try, no matter what our backgrounds, we are going to make mistakes. Much to my dismay, I make mistakes when I know better. My children could tell you some of my errors better than I could (I only pray none of them decide to write a book on that subject one day!).

God can override our mistakes. Remember, He works in the lives of our children as well as in our lives. Your abortion will not adversely affect your mothering ability unless you permit it to do so.

Will I abuse my living children?

It is interesting to learn that contrary to popular pro-abortion arguments which say unwanted, unaborted babies are likely to become victims of abuse, studies indicate aborted women abuse their children more frequently than those who have not aborted.[7]

"Some parents become so frightened of their own rage, they withdraw from involvement with their children or leave

---

6. Please don't confuse overprotection with genuine concern for your children's safety and well-being.
7. Dr. and Mrs. J. C. Willke, *Abortion: Questions and Answers,* rev. ed. (Hayes Publishing Company, Inc., Cincinnati, 1988), pp. 141–44; Dr. Philip G. Ney, "A Consideration of Abortion Survivors," *Child Psychiatry and Human Development,* Vol. 13(3), Spring 1983, p. 172.

home. Others enact that destructive rage, which may injure their children, maim or kill them. In all creatures, a signal of helpless distress from the young will invite either parental care or aggression. . . . A woman, to abort her helpless young, must overcome her instinctual impulse to attend to the little one's helplessness. Having done so once, it may be easier the next time."[8]

When a child cries out in distress, a mother's natural inclination is to find out what the problem is and remedy it. Once we have killed a baby, unconsciously we may view anything less than murder (such as anger or physical abuse) as acceptable.

"Child abusers cannot be easily categorized. Battery occurs because of maladjusted attitudes, not because of poverty or ignorance. It is clearly not confined to any social or economic class."[9] Maladjusted attitudes include unresolved guilt and anger in your own life. In other words, any person has the potential to become a child abuser.

That's the bad news. The exciting news is that you *can* beat the odds and become a loving, nurturing mother.

We once thought unborn babies were of value only to the degree they were "wanted." Our opinion of our unborn baby's value determined our treatment of him. This attitude was wrong and we know it now. Each person—born or unborn—has intrinsic value that is unaltered by what we think. If we view each child as valuable and precious, our desire will be to cherish and nurture him.

8. Dr. Philip G. Ney, "Relationship between Abortion and Child Abuse," *Canadian Journal of Psychiatry,* Vol. 24, No. 7 (1979), p. 612.
9. David C. Reardon, *Aborted Women—Silent No More* (Good News Publishers, Crossway Books, Westchester, Illinois, 1988), p. 224.

How can I make sure my abortion will not adversely affect my child rearing?

Accept your aborted baby as dead. Don't allow your dead baby to destroy your relationship with your living children. This is one reason why grieving must come to an end.

Seek a balance in your relationship with your living children. Understand that your children do not exist to meet your needs—they exist to fulfill God's plan for their lives.

Anger toward children reflects our selfishness at not having what we expected or wanted. We may be tired or ill. We may want to be doing something other than mothering. We may begrudge our child time we must spend with him. What would our reaction be if we looked at the problem from our child's point of view?

Because I am task-oriented, my tendency is to push aside my kids when I'm involved in a project. This has nothing to do with my abortion. It reflects my basic personality. I have learned to put aside my work to meet the needs of my children. It's not easy, but it's rewarding!

Philippians 2:3–4 admonishes us, "Do nothing out of selfish ambition or vain conceit, but in humility consider others better than yourselves. Each of you should look not only to your own interests, but also to the interests of others" (NIV). If we view each person as of higher value than ourselves and our wants, we will be not only better mothers but better human beings.

Know your limits. Raising children is stressful. Their demands often seem to surpass our ability to meet them. It has taken me a while to understand that when I am harsh and impatient with my children, this is not a result of my abortion but a result of my sinful response to a stressful situation. When I explode, they are not to blame. I am. Don't take your frustrations out on your kids. Take your anger to God and resolve it before correcting your children's behavior.

Meditate on God's words regarding mothering:

> Behold, children are a *gift* of the Lord; The fruit of the womb is a *reward.* (Psalms 127:3)

> He settles the barren woman in her home as a *happy mother* of children. Praise the Lord. (Psalms 113:9 NIV)

Can any positive effect result from my abortion with respect to mothering?

We have learned much about ourselves, our God, and our close relationships because of our experience with abortion. We will continue to grow and learn. Because of this, we can become better mothers than we thought possible.

Because we understand God's great love for *us* and forgiveness of our sins, we are in an excellent position to show our children how much we love *them.* In our daily lives we can demonstrate sacrificial love that puts aside our own desires (and even our needs) to meet our child's need.

Yes, positive consequences can result from your abortion experience.

Two women share their thoughts:

> I now feel very strongly that every conception is a gift from God and that He would want us to treat it as such. I feel abortion is a terrible thing in this society—another black area in our lives that keeps us from living the way God intended us to live. I am now strong enough in those beliefs again that I feel more confident as a mother, on how to counsel my daughters regarding sex, conception and birth control. (Liz)

> I know that in bringing three beautiful sons in my life [God] gives me comfort and peace in living with my

"secret" of ten years ago. I will be more caring and loving with my sons because of this. (Anonymous)

Now turn to the quotation that begins this chapter. Decide by an act of your will to make it true in your life.

CHAPTER TWENTY-ONE

Will I Ever Be Completely Healed?

"Even tho' I've forgiven myself and accepted God's grace, there is still a hurt in my heart."

Anonymous

Learning to live with the choice you made sometimes takes more time than you wish. There is a saying that "time heals all wounds." I would argue that time may cause us to ignore the wound—we may believe it to be healed. Underneath the surface a potential hotbed of infection could be brewing. Healing takes more than the passage of time. Proper treatment is essential.

What does it mean to be completely healed?

For us who have submitted to abortions, the question is not "Is abortion wrong?" The question we ask is "How do I live with the wrong I've done by aborting my baby?" We found that although abortion is a terribly wrong act, healing can occur. That healing can become complete. However, complete healing will never include forgetting. Teri Reisser correctly states that our "painful memories cannot ever be fully erased, only fully faced and put into proper perspective."[1] The memory will fade with time, but part of our abortion will forever remain with us. That's good. We need to remember God's graciousness in forgiving us so great a sin. We also need to remember our experience because it can affect positively our dealing with other people when we recall what we have been through.

Right now, as I'm writing this chapter, if I dwelled on my abortion—the horribleness, the tragedy, the cruelty of my sin of abortion—I could fall into a deep depression. It is only by *refusing* to dwell on my past and its sin that I go forward, usable to God for His purposes. Christ alone holds me together (Colossians 1:17), and only by leaning on His strength moment by moment do I remain whole and healed.

Jesus is our hope for going on—for facing our problems and dealing with them one by one, once and for all. "I *can* do *all* things through Him [Christ] who strengthens me" (Philippians 4:13). Victory is ours for the asking!

I still find it very difficult to see films on abortion—or to get into extensive conversations. Is that normal?

Wendy answers this question:

Viewing pictures makes me uncomfortable somewhat and again I think this is a normal response to violence. At the same time I also want to know and see articles and pictures on abortion because this information is vital in knowing the truth about abortion and its consequences.

I believe abortion will likely always be painful to

1. Teri K. Reisser, notes from post-abortion seminar, Open ARMs convention, May 1987.

discuss or read about but I mean that in its best sense. Knowing the pain of the children who will be "choiced" from this [earth] and the women who will choose and the pain that will follow for them makes abortion painful for me. In situations when I am revealing my experience it is uncomfortable and painful for me but I believe this to be a normal human response to self disclosure of any kind.

Can I ever get rid of the pain I have when I watch *The Silent Scream* and the like? I fall apart. Other times I'm okay.

No human being with normal emotions could watch *The Silent Scream* and not react internally and/or outwardly to it. Teenagers, men, and women who have not personally experienced abortion cry. Miscarried women cry. Aborted women cry whether they are healed or not. If they don't cry outwardly, they feel a pain deep inside that says, "You did this." If they are healed they think, "But thank God, I am forgiven."

We don't want to become so "healed" that we are numb to the pain that abortion inflicts.

Why can't I trust God to heal me?

A lady writes, "I want to be free, but at the same time I'm afraid to let go." Problems that people don't resolve are a result of failure to follow God's methods and instructions. We become used to doing things our own way, the way that makes logical sense to us. Trusting God involves faith. Hebrews 11:1 defines faith as "the substance of things hoped for, the evidence of things not seen (KJV)." Dr. Charles Ryrie comments, "Faith gives reality and proof of things unseen, treating them as if they were already objects of sight

193

rather than of hope."[2] We are asked to trust the unseen God with our lives, our souls, and our hopes. Faith is essential for us to keep working through our problems (Job 19:25–27). Patricia L. Tompkins comments, "I now walk in the full forgiveness of Christ. I realized last fall that my greatest sin still in my life was not accepting God's full forgiveness. I was guilty of not walking in faith. I am happy now for the first time in seventeen years. I am free."

Jesus the carpenter took raw materials and hewed and carved them into beautifully completed workmanship. Christ the Savior takes the raw material of human potential and builds into us the beauty and functionality of a finely finished Christian. We are His workmanship (Ephesians 2:10). Let Jesus Christ complete the work He has begun in you.

Does the Lord want to use me in this area to help others? Or does He care enough about me to just heal me?

This twofold question implies that God may not care enough to heal people unless they commit themselves to be used of God in the area in which they are healed. We have found that God does love you enough to forgive you completely for your sin of abortion. Healing takes place as we apply biblical principles to our wounds. However, once healed, many women desire to help others out of gratitude for what God has done for them.

Can anything match the shame and humiliation of the perfect Christ dying on a cross for our sins? Just as Christ chose to die to free us, so we can choose to speak the truth to free others. Outward extension of ministry to others done at the prompting of the Holy Spirit indicates our inner healing is complete. This may mean speaking to only one other woman

2. Dr. Charles Caldwell Ryrie, *The Ryrie Study Bible; New American Standard Translation* (Moody Press, Chicago, 1978), footnote p. 1850.

whom God brings your way to receive love and understanding. God does not call every aborted woman to a public ministry. Teri Reisser puts it well: "The woman who has experienced healing will find herself willing (though not necessarily eager) to share her story in any situation where she judges the hearer(s) will benefit from her narrative."[3]

A friend recently shared with me the beauty of Deuteronomy 32:11 and Exodus 19:4. Here we see the example of a mother eagle stirring up her young and moving them out of the nest when they are ready to learn to fly. She then swoops down and catches them on her outspread wing before they can fall and injure themselves. She allows them out on their own only when they are fully prepared to fly. The young eagles attempt to fly because they have faith their mother will be there for them if they should falter. God won't ask you to "fly" until you are ready.

Will I ever be a "normal" person again?

Much philosophical rhetoric could be spent defining "normal." For purposes of this book, "normal" means you can discuss abortion, view films and pictures, and live your private life with inner calm and outward composure. It does *not* mean you will never cry or feel regret. As Judy Schmid says, "I still cry, but that's okay. I don't want to lose my sensitivity." Yes, you can be "normal" again!

I have so many PAS symptoms. Will I ever resolve them all?

Women have latched on to the term "post-abortion syndrome" (PAS) because it offers tangible evidence that abortions cause genuine problems. Personally, I prefer the term

3. Teri and Dr. Paul Reisser, *Help for the Post-abortion Woman* (Zondervan Publishing House, Grand Rapids, 1989), pp. 82–83.

"post-abortion trauma" because many women do not have a syndrome, but simply a few problems they need to deal with once and for all. The word "syndrome" gives the impression of a continuing cycle of adverse emotional reactions. "Trauma," on the other hand, indicates an injury that can be treated and will one day heal. The right treatment is vital to complete healing.

You see, the emotional upheaval which occurs following an abortion is a spiritual problem. That is, abortion's emotional aftermath results from sinful responses to various emotions that rise up within us. I suggest that the term "sin-drome" would be the *most* appropriate term to use![4] Once women begin to deal with problems God's way, using His proven methods, healing completes itself—the guilt, fear, grief, anger, shame disperse. Looking for and identifying symptoms may help you understand where you are in the healing process, but remember to focus your eyes on God who can heal you. As one woman writes, "You can talk about it, cry, fellowship, go to shrinks, but without Jesus there is NO peace."

I feel that I have victory over the guilt; then if I read some abortion material or watch something abortion-related, I find myself dealing with another layer of healing. Why?

Your healing process does not complete itself overnight. But be encouraged, for God never allows you to face more than you can handle at one time (1 Corinthians 10:13). Once you successfully resolve one problem area regarding your abortion, God may introduce another in order to further your growth as a Christian. If treated properly, eventually all the layers of hurt will heal.

4. Debbie Marshall, coauthor of the *In His Image* Bible study, uses the term "post-abortion consequences" because the problems we face are *consequences* of a sinful action in our lives.

Let me give you an illustration. Two times I cut my little finger. The first time I applied pressure to stop the bleeding and then put a bandage over the wound. The wound became infected and never healed properly. To this day I have a painful scar reminding me I didn't get the proper help when it was needed. The second time I cut my finger, I immediately went to the emergency room of the hospital. There the doctor cleansed the wound, applied antiseptic, and stitched the gaping hole. That wound healed properly. You can barely see the scar, and the pain is gone. That is the result of properly treating a wound.

Now think of your abortion as an open, gaping wound. You can use the do-it-yourself method, or you can go to the Great Physician Jesus Christ for healing. His instruction manual, the Bible, will guide you on necessary treatment for your wound. Complete healing will result when you follow His instructions carefully. Abortion is a terrible wound. It can and will heal, but a tiny scar will remain to remind you that you once hurt.

There seem to be times now when I can talk about it and not get upset, but does that mean I no longer care about what I did?

Only you know your heart, but I would guess this is a good sign that you are healing. I like the attitude of Jill Iversen as she comments, "I will continue to learn from and benefit from this for the rest of my life." Don't allow yourself to feel guilty because you no longer feel guilty about your abortion. It is normal for the negative emotions to pass as you resolve your problems. Don't fear acceptance of your abortion. Acceptance and peace indicate the healing is complete.

I kept a journal which started about three or four months before the abortion, and I continued writing up to a year or so after. I am thinking of burning it or burying it as a sign of putting the abortion behind me. Is that morose or escapist?

Committing our thoughts to paper can help clarify our thinking, preserves memories, and gets it out of our systems. Many people keep diaries or journals. Writing down our thoughts and perceptions gives us a subjectively viewed written record of our lives.

I think the record of your abortion *should* be destroyed when you are done with it. Burning your diary is like putting a stake in the ground to mark a momentous occasion: My abortion is over and done with. It is part of my past . . . just like this record. Now it is physically gone, retained in my memory, but not actively part of my daily thoughts.

An exception would be if you plan to write or speak about your experience. Your diary would prove invaluable for recalling specific incidents, dates, and thoughts. If you plan to keep your diary and are not yet going public about your abortion, please put it in a safety-deposit box or other place for safe-keeping.

What are the steps to complete healing?[5]

Healing involves changing the way we think and act. God has the answer to *any* problem you face, but you must change in order to apply the solution to your life.

The following six steps are essential for complete healing:

5. Much of the text of this section is from Pam Koerbel, *Abortion's Second Victim* (Victor Books, Wheaton, Illinois, 1986), pp. 164–65.

1. Recognize your areas of sin (1 John 1:8).
2. Repent of your sin (1 John 1:9).
3. Request God's help, depending upon Him to hear you (1 John 5:14–15).
4. Relinquish your sinful thoughts or actions (Romans 6:5–7; Colossians 3:8–9).
5. Replace your sinful thoughts or actions with a godly response (Colossians 3:10; Romans 12:1–2).
6. Repeat the above five steps until your godly response becomes a habit (John 3:21; Colossians 3:23).

Remember—*before* you take these six steps, you must first accept Christ's atonement on your behalf. Until you come by faith to trust Christ as your personal Savior, all attempts to overcome your abortion aftermath are done in your own strength. Resolving abortion's aftermath completely and permanently is accomplished through God's power and only if you are His child.

I fully realize the methods of dealing with your abortion presented in this book are contrary to the way the world would have you deal with your abortion. Without the Holy Spirit to guide you, the solutions I've presented would appear foolish, and you would not understand why they will work. As you begin to practice God's solutions, you will find they *do* work.

Galatians 5:19–21 contains a list of things that God hates. Included are immorality, impurity, enmities, strife, jealousy, outbursts of anger, disputes, and envying. These are the things we practiced in the past but now desire to eliminate from our lives.

As you begin to deal with your sinful emotional responses to your abortion in a way pleasing to God, the Holy Spirit will begin to produce fruit in your life. Galatians 5:22–23 lists nine parts to the fruit of the Holy Spirit: love, joy, peace, patience, kindness, goodness, faithfulness, gentleness, and self-control. These result from proper responses to emotions that once overwhelmed you to the point of despair. Look for this fruit in your life as you begin to solve your problems God's way.

Your natural tendency will be to return to your negative thought patterns. You may be encouraged to go your own way by people who may ridicule you as you apply biblical principles to your life. Expect it, but don't allow ungodly attitudes and advice to keep you from having victory over your problems. Understand that "the message of the cross is foolishness to those who are perishing, but to us who are being saved it is the power of God" (1 Corinthians 1:18 NIV).

Where do I go from here?

Judy Bates shares this:

> Even as a Christian in the beginning I battled with the abortion issue. It must be okay, its legal, its my body, my life, the practical thing to do. It took a couple of years to realize the conflict of humanism to God's Word and which one is truth. I confessed to God and asked His forgiveness. Mentally, through the promise of God's Word, I knew it was done. But emotionally it has not been so easy. . . . [After learning about abortion and its alternatives] I've experienced more hurting in the last six months! Praise God! I'm still hurting! But I know that I am coming along, and that this is a part of the grieving and healing process.

This gal is serious about working through her problem. She has read books, talked to an Open ARMs counselor, thought about her abortion, told her ten-year-old daughter because she plans to become active in pro-life, and confessed to a group of three close Christian friends. She prays daily "for God to use me and heal me to a point where I can be used through this experience without becoming so emotional that I'm not functional." She also is opening her home as a support home for women in crisis pregnancy. By focusing on others, she will soon reach out and give back what she has learned.

Abortion was the wrong choice. You know that now. It may have been made from outside pressure or from selfishness. The reason for the choice is behind you. You face the present and future with the reality of living with your choice. Now you have another choice. You can push your abortion into the recesses of your mind, hoping it will fade away and cease to haunt your waking and sleeping moments, or you can deal with it once and for all—get it settled in your mind, every detail and aspect of it. Work it through, then walk away from it. There is only one choice that will bring you peace and freedom. The choice is yours—what will you do?

I Can Go On

They ask me if I feel the pain
From a sin of long ago;
The answer's "Yes, I feel the pain
And tears sometimes still flow."
My sin was that I took a life
Innocent, unborn, my child's.
For years I carried guilt and grief
That I had been beguiled—
That I had cared for self so much
My baby had to die;
And day and night I tossed and turned
Wishing it had been I.
Then I met Someone who could pay
A debt I never could
His name is Jesus, Son of God—
Pure, sinless, holy, good.
He paid my debt and set me free
Despair no more is mine,
For Jesus holds me tight with arms
That ease my pain with time.

Chorus:
I can go on with Jesus at my side
I can go on my sin no more to hide;
I can go on to live in victory
Because one day my Savior set me free.[6]

CHAPTER TWENTY-TWO

How Can I Help Others Avoid the Same Mistake?

"I feel that maybe my story could be used to help a woman know she doesn't have to go through all I went through. There is hope and his name is Jesus."

Anonymous

Aborted women suffer—of that we are certain. When the abortion laws are reversed and/or the medical profession finally admits the reality of post-abortion trauma, two things will happen:

1. Women by the thousands (perhaps millions) will begin to seek help because they will realize they have done something wrong which they *thought* was right because it was legal, and/or they will realize their inner turmoil and feelings of guilt are genuine.
2. Many will seek help in the wrong places unless we reach them first.

The implications are awesome and far-reaching.

Would I be a help to someone like me who has gone through abortion?

People need love and healing. They need healing because they hurt. They need love, compassion, and forgiveness in order to heal. They need someone to tell them how to be forgiven and get on with their lives.

My friend, you have no idea how many women are yearning for another aborted woman with whom they can talk. Although I believe that a person does not have to experience something in order to help, I know that if you have gone through a particular situation, doors readily open for you to help another. Because you have had an abortion, other aborted women know you will understand their pain, guilt, and grief. They know you will keep what you hear in confidence. Most of all, an aborted woman coming to you for help finds hope as she sees and hears that you are healed.

In addition to being a listening ear and offering wise counsel, you can offer help in another very needed and practical way. In a crisis situation a person needs to concentrate on getting the major problem resolved. Facets of everyday life can become major obstacles to working through the problem. A woman may need extended periods of time alone to pray, study, or seek counsel. Most likely, she would be glad of your offer to baby-sit, help with housework, fix a meal—anything you can think of to alleviate her load so she can concentrate on resolving her problem. That's love in action!

How do I find other aborted women?

When I had my abortion in 1971, women were just beginning to "take advantage" of legalized abortion in New York State. I knew no other women who had submitted to an abortion. Women weren't talking. The only reason my abortion was not secret was that the father had spread the news across campus in a effort to convince people that he was not the father. Eleven years after my abortion, I finally met another aborted woman. It was by accident that I found out her secret. One of my closest friends, she had had an abortion several years previously. For the first time, I had someone who could really understand what I'd gone through.

Since that time I have met hundreds of aborted women and have heard from hundreds more by phone and letter. The only reason I know so many aborted women is because I write and speak on the subject. Just as most of us tried to keep our abortions secret, so millions of other aborted women keep their secret well hidden too.

In the past year or two, locating aborted women has become easier. Women are slowly beginning to come forth to receive the help they need. Groups such as Open ARMs, WEBA, and American Victims of Abortion encourage women to come forward to get help in resolving their post-abortion problems. I encourage you to participate in a post-abortion support group or Bible study. There are now several books on the subject which assist women to come to terms with their action.

As women heal, they often voluntarily come forward to help others. Phyllis Lefort writes, "The Lord has already opened doors for me to share on a one-to-one basis with a few women and I was amazed how easy it is when I know it is in His timing and with the right person."

Now that I see abortion for what it is, what can I do about it?

There are several avenues available for effective work in both the pro-life and post-abortion areas. Regina shares her work: "I go every other Saturday morning and stand for two hours on the sidewalk in front of the abortion mill where my first child was killed, and try to talk to the women before they go in. I offer whatever help they need to let their babies live; as well as pray. Sometimes they turn away; usually they don't. I also write to all my elected officials and try to get them to shape our laws according to the pro-life beliefs of the majority of their constituents."

Following is a list of ways you might help. You're certain to find an area that suits your particular talents and gifts:

- One-on-one sharing as the Lord opens doors
- Lay (or professional, if you have a desire to study for a degree) counseling at crisis pregnancy centers, for post-abortion groups, or privately
- Contacting legislators by phone and/or letter to make your beliefs known (each of us should be doing this!)
- Lobbying
- Working hot lines
- Leading a support group or Bible study
- Demonstrations such as Operation Rescue (you can picket, sit in, counsel, or simply be there to sing and pray)
- Writing articles and/or books addressing the topic of abortion
- Public speaking in schools, churches, rallies, and the like (groups are always on the lookout for a good speaker with an interesting and current topic)
- Radio and television interviews
- Financial support for post-abortion work and crisis pregnancy groups
- Prayer (this is one area each of us should practice regularly because all the preceding will be in vain without God's help)

I've never prepared a speech. What should I include?

Stick to the central issue—abortion kills babies and leaves the mother with physical and/or emotional problems. People need to know certain facts, some of which follow:

- Life begins at conception.
- Statistics on the development of an unborn baby (such as, the baby is distinguishable at eight weeks as a human being, his heart begins beating at twenty-four days, his skeleton is formed at forty-two days, and the like) which provide graphic and concrete evidence of human life in the womb (I often use photographs of unborn babies during this part of my presentation).
- Abortion is the most common elective surgery in the United States.
- Abortion is legal the entire nine months of pregnancy.[1]
- Methods used to perform abortions (including a hesterotomy, which is the same procedure as a Caesarian section, but is the term used for late-term abortions).
- Thirty percent of previously aborted women call for help during a subsequent pregnancy.
- Abortion causes women physical and/or emotional problems (see Chapter 2 for listing).
- Four thousand abortions are performed daily (I usually mention that during the half hour I speak, almost one hundred babies die from abortion).

You will be surprised by the number of people who do not know the basic facts regarding abortion. Aborted women's silence, coupled with pro-abortion propaganda, has done a thorough job of hiding the truth. People can't pass on the truth to others until they know and understand it themselves.[2]

Additionally, tell what God has done for you. Include where you were before God found you (lost and in despair), what God did for you (salvation), and where you are now in your life (healed and sharing the truth). People *want* to hear

1. As of the writing of this book, three cases are pending before the U. S. Supreme Court which could severely limit or overturn the *Roe vs. Wade* decision of 1973.
2. Always have pro-life and post-abortion literature available when you speak.

your personal story. No one can tell your story and touch people with it as you can.[3]

Can you give a sample testimony?

Speak from your heart. My pastor made a comment which has profoundly affected my approach to people, especially regarding giving my abortion testimony: "People don't care how much you know, until they know how much you care."

A testimony might go like this one, quoted in full from a woman who wrote to me:

He Set Me Free

I've never told my story publicly so I hope you'll bear with me. I'd like to tell you a little bit about my life. My mother and father had 12 children and I was number 12. My father died when I was 2 years old. My mother did the best she knew how raising all of us by herself. My family doesn't show or express affection, so I guess I sort of felt lost in the crowd.

I wanted someone to hold me and love me so much— I ached for it. At the time I didn't realize how much God loved me. I started dating a certain guy when I was 16 and soon after confused making love with being loved. So at the very young age of 17 I found myself pregnant.

I felt so all alone in the world and so unloved. All I heard from my doctor and friends was, "it's only tissue, have an abortion, get it over with and no one will know." A close friend had just had an abortion and she kept pressuring me too.

I *never* once heard, "it's a baby, how about adoption or

3. It may not always be possible to speak of God and Christ. When you're speaking in a public school, for example, this would not be permitted. However, you can encourage people to speak with you afterward. When they approach you privately, you can share Christ with them.

208

about the deep pain and emotional scars that abortion causes." I wrestled with this decision but since I wasn't given any positive information or wasn't raised with any knowledge that this was right or wrong—I chose abortion.

Now I don't mean to sound like this was their fault because it was my decision. But I believe if I would have had counseling from a Crisis Pregnancy Center I would not have made the decision that I did.

Since I was only seventeen I had to have my mother's permission, which she gave and it was never discussed again. You see if it wasn't something you could laugh about it wasn't discussed.

So I graduated from high school one month pregnant and an emotional mess. The night before my abortion I was extremely depressed. I was with friends at a park. They were off having a good time as I sat by the water on that warm beautiful star-lit night. It was like something out of a painting.

As I sat mulling it over and over in my head, I couldn't believe what was about to take place—it was a very bad dream. I sat and fought for hours with God. Oh how I didn't want to have that abortion. My whole body and mind screamed NO! But I didn't know why I didn't want to have this abortion and all I could think of is—I have no other choice—I have to.

That day in June of 1974 was the worst day of my life. It was a day I would live to regret daily.

The doctor and nurse had no compassion for me. They were rushing through the procedure so they could get someone else in there. The doctor made a very crude remark to me that cut like a knife in my heart. I received no pre or post abortion counseling. From that day on I was never the same.

I had such pain and guilt in my heart I thought I would go crazy. I had absolutely no self esteem. I grieved for my lost baby, but I had to push it down and out of my mind because I was the cause of my baby's death. I briefly contemplated suicide but thank God I was too scared.

So here I was feeling unlovable but within a year God sent me my husband. Only God could have sent me a man as sensitive, loving and understanding as Bruce and at the perfect time.

So a year later we were married but my problems didn't stop there. I still had guilt, low self esteem and physical pain—all caused from my abortion. I lived with this for over ten years—eating away at me.

Then I met Jesus Christ and He changed my life. He became my personal Lord and Savior and God forgave me for *all* my sins including my abortion. He not only forgave my sins, He forgot them!

I believe God forgave me that November day in 1984 but I didn't forgive myself. I still held guilt and disbelief that I could do such a terrible thing.

Well that would take almost 3 more years for me to be rid of. One summer day in 1987 when I was working at the CPC, Gretchen [the director] was the counselor and I was the client. She prayed for an inner healing to take place in my life and God granted that prayer. Praise God —He set me free once and for all from that sin that held me in bondage for years!

He took away the guilt and pain but I still have a sadness and regret for what I did. I thank God for how He has turned my life around. I thank Him for the two beautiful children He has blessed me with. God has made Romans 8:28 very real to me.

I have been sharing my experience at the CPC with abortion-minded girls. I felt led to reveal this to you so I can be even more effective in helping more girls say no to abortion and yes to life for their babies. And I believe through all of this God will be glorified.

In conclusion I would just like to say the Crisis Pregnancy Center isn't just for young pregnant girls. It's for people like me who want to help but first need help themselves.

God took a horrible thing in my life and turned it around to be used for good. If God can use me He can certainly use you. It's not what we can do, it's what we can let God do through us.

The Lord has touched many lives through this ministry including mine and I praise Him for that.[4]

What do I do when my counsel fails to change someone's mind?

This is an important question for you to consider. What will *your* reaction be if someone has an abortion after you have counseled them against it? What if a woman you counsel fails to apply biblical principles to her life in order to heal? What if you must watch a friend go slowly "down the tubes" because she continues to deny she did anything wrong in having an abortion? How will it affect *you?*

Each woman makes her own choice in response to a particular situation or piece of advice. You are responsible for speaking the truth in love. The guilt for failing to follow sound advice rests not with you but with the other person.

Will I ever see any good coming out of this?

Thousands of women's lives have already been changed for the better because of their abortion experience. They are more compassionate, more caring, more patient, more focused on serving others, and more forgiving than before their abortions.

I believe some of us must experience the depths of despair

4. Debbie K. Weiser, speech given at the Delaware Crisis Pregnancy Center banquet, Delaware, Ohio, Spring, 1988.

before we will turn to God. Only then will we permit God access to our lives and hearts. Your abortion may be what turned your life around and caused you to realize you needed Christ to forgive your sins. We are told, "In everything give thanks; for this is God's will for you in Christ Jesus" (1 Thessalonians 5:18). Thank God for your abortion if it brought you to Him. In this sense it served a "good" purpose.

How do I make it right?

We've discussed previously that you can never make right your abortion. However, you can show God's love to others by sharing what has happened in your life. Second Corinthians 5:15 tells us we should live for others because of what Christ did for us. Read how and why some women respond:

> Sharing has been relatively easy. This is my first opportunity to share with a person I don't know personally [reference to letter she wrote to me] and that can sometimes be scary, but I do trust God and I know He honors my sharing. And as terrible as my sin was, if others have access to my experience and that of others and they decide on the side of life then glory to God—He does indeed use all things for good (Romans 8:28). Luke 7:47 speaks of the connection between forgiveness of sins and love. Those forgiven much have much love to give. I have been forgiven much therefore I must have much love to give and I'd best be obedient and share that—to His glory. (Wendy)

> I am so glad to share my feelings if it will help. I don't want anyone to go through the pain of the procedure itself or the agonizing aftereffects. My only strength has been my relationship with Jesus. He has truly forgiven me, and has shown me so much love. (Miyoshi)

I understand why I chose to have an abortion at that time in my life. I wish I would have been able to look at the other options seriously, but I was running out of time. I feel the need to help other teenagers and women who are faced with a similar situation. I do feel good about who I am today and where my life is going! (Anonymous)

Let me offer three cautions as you begin to reach out to others. One, don't go public because you "feel" you must to atone for your guilt in aborting your baby. Nancy Michels puts it so well: "A woman is ready to make a commitment to the pro-life ministry when she comes forward not out of guilt but from freewill and healed conviction."[5] You will know you are ready when you are nervous but at peace and when God clearly opens the door. Two, don't try to help others until you have learned to apply biblical principles to your own life and are completely healed. Women who are not yet healed often unknowingly transfer their anger, bitterness, and turmoil to other women. Three, don't try to help others in your own strength. Even Jesus took time to fast, pray, and meditate because He knew that power comes from God, not from our inner selves. Post-abortion work is extremely stressful, and burn-out is a very real possibility. Always bathe your work in prayer, relying totally on God to work *through* you. I keep a little quote over my kitchen sink which reads, ". . . what makes a person valuable is not what he is able to do, but what God is able to do through him."[6]

The words of the apostle Paul in 1 Corinthians 15:10 also have special meaning for me: "But by the grace of God I am what I am, and His grace toward me did not prove vain; but I

5. Nancy Michels, *Helping Women Recover from Abortion* (Bethany House Publishers, Minneapolis, 1988), p. 148.
6. Miltinnie Yih, title unknown of article in *Kindred Spirit,* Dallas, Texas, Winter 1986.

labored even more than all of them, yet not I, but the grace of God with me."

There is so much I've wanted to tell you. There are so many questions and no easy answers. These pages only touch the surface of my heart's desire—that you may go forth in your life healed and whole, having cast your burden upon Jesus, committed to helping others in whatever way He leads.

Each hand reaching out to touch and hold another hand strengthens the chain as we weld links so strong that no power can break them. Join with those of us who are healed. Reach out your hand and touch a hurting life. Pass on what you have learned. Someone needs your love, your compassion, the understanding only you can bring to her. Someone reached out to you. Aren't you glad that person did?

If I can help you in any way, please contact me. I love you so very much.

Pam

Pam Koerbel
c/o Post Abortion Ministries
P.O. Box 3092
Landover Hills, Maryland 20784-0092

Appendixes

Note: The following organizations and literature are listed for your information. Pam Koerbel does not necessarily endorse each in its entirety. Please evaluate them in light of what God declares to be true in the Holy Bible (Acts 17:11b).

APPENDIX A

Post-abortion Support Groups

United States

American Victims of Abortion
  Olivia Gans, Director
  419 Seventh Street, N.W., Suite 500
  Washington, D.C. 20004
  (202) 626-8800

CARE (Counseling for Abortion Related Experiences)
  Marjorie Becker, Executive Director
  709B Investment Building
  Pittsburgh, Pennsylvania 15222
  (412) 572-5099

Christian Action Council (United States and Canada)
  PACE Program (Post Abortion Counseling and Education)
  101 W. Broad Street, Suite 500
  Falls Church, Virginia 22046
  (703) 237-2100

Come Alive Ministries
  318 High Street
  Morgantown, West Virginia 26505
  (304) 296-1111

Conquerors
  Julie Gehrke, Director
  435 Aldine, Suite 201
  St. Paul, Minnesota 55104
  (612) 641-5595

Heart to Heart
  Sue Liljenberg, Executive Director
  P.O. Box 7652
  Federal Way, Washington 98003
  (206) 839-4525

Open ARMs (Abortion Related Ministries)
  Jim and Patti Goodoien, National Directors
  P.O. Box 19835
  Indianapolis, Indiana 46219
  (317) 359-9950

Post Abortion Ministries
  Pam Koerbel, Ministries Coordinator
  P.O. Box 3092
  Landover HIlls, Maryland 20784-0092
  (301) 773-4630

Project Rachel
  National Office of Post-Abortion Reconciliation and Healing, Inc.
  Vicki Thorn, Executive Director
  St. John Center
  3680 S. Kinnickinnic Avenue
  Milwaukee, Wisconsin 53207
  (800) 5WE-CARE

Victims of Choice
  Nola Jones, Executive Director
  124 Shefield Drive
  Vacaville, California 95687
  (707) 448-6015

Walls Evaporate, Blessings Abound
  Carla J. Smith, Director
  4900 Glenway Avenue
  Cincinnati, Ohio 45238
  (513) 921-9322

WEBA (Women Exploited by Abortion)
  Kathy Walker, National President
  3553 B North Perris Boulevard, Suite 4
  Perris, California 92370
  (714) 657-0334

Canadian

Abortion Crisis Centre
  Beverly Hadland, Executive Director
  219 Dufferin Street, Suite 200A
  Toronto, Ontario M6K 1Z1
  (416) 535-5135 or 1586

Canadian Victims of Abortion
  Box 2
  Stewart Valley, Saskatchewan S0N 2P0
  (306) 778-3625

PAST (Post-Abortion Support Teams)
  215 Talfourd Street
  Sarnia, Ontario N7T 1N9
  (519) 332-4438

British

British Victims of Abortion S.P.U.C.
  7 Tufton Street
  London, England SW1P 3QN

APPENDIX B

Additional Reading

Books

Koerbel, Pam. *Abortion's Second Victim.* Victor Books, 1825 College Avenue, Wheaton, Illinois 60187 (1986). Tells of the horror of abortion firsthand and shows how people struggling with abortion's aftermath can find forgiveness and peace.

Mannion, Fr. Michael T. *Abortion and Healing: A Cry to Be Whole.* Sheed and Ward, 115 East Armour Boulevard, P.O. Box 281, Kansas City, Missouri 64141-0281 (1986). Offers insights into compassionately responding to women who have experienced an abortion.

Michels, Nancy. *Helping Women Recover from Abortion.* Bethany House Publishers, 6820 Auto Club Road, Minneapolis, Minnesota 55438 (1988). Explains the grieving process aborted women pass through and offers biblical solutions for restoration.

Reardon, David C. *Aborted Women—Silent No More.* Good News Publishers, Crossway Books, 9825 West Roosevelt Road, Westchester, Illinois 60153 (1987). Based on a survey of women involved with WEBA (Women Exploited by Abortion); includes case studies.

Reisser, Teri and Dr. Paul. *Help for the Post-abortion Woman.* Zondervan Publishing House, 1415 Lake Drive S.E., Grand Rapids, Michigan 49506 (1989). For women who are suffering (or think they may be suffering) from abortion's emotional aftermath, and for family, friends, and counselors who desire to help women with PAS.

Shettles, Dr. Landrum, and Rorvik, David. *Rites of Life.* Zondervan Publishing House, 1415 Lake Drive S.E., Grand Rapids, Michigan 49506 (1983). Excellent work on the existence of human life from the moment of conception; includes photographs.

Wilkes, Peter. *Overcoming Anger & Other Dragons of the Soul.* InterVarsity Press, P.O. Box 1400, Downers Grove, Illinois 60515 (1987). Written to help you break loose from persistent sins (such as guilt, anger, lust, doubt); includes good thought questions at the end of each chapter.

Willke, Dr. and Mrs. J. C. *Abortion: Questions and Answers.* Revised edition. Hayes Publishing Company, Inc., 6304 Hamilton Avenue, Cincinnati, Ohio 45224 (1988). Clearly and concisely answers questions concerning an unborn baby's development and abortion; includes photographs.

Pamphlets

Abortion: Where Have All the Babies Gone? Pamphlet # R131. American Tract Society, Box 462008, Garland, Texas 75046-2008. A brief history and look at the issues that led to the decision of *Roe v. Wade.*

. . . But I Can't Forgive Myself! Last Days Ministries, Box 40, Lindale, Texas 75771-0040.

Forgotten Fathers: Men and Abortion. Life Cycle Books, P.O. Box 792, Lewiston, New York 14092-0792.

Healing the Pain of Abortion. Pamphlet # PT183M. Paper Treasures, 216 Glen, Iowa Falls, Iowa 50126.

Hope for Today—Healing After Abortion. Open ARMs, P.O. Box 19835, Indianapolis, Indiana 46219.

Life Before Birth. Pamphlet # 7K06. Good News Publishers, 9825 West Roosevelt Road, Westchester, Illinois 60153. Highlights milestones in the development of an unborn baby.

No More Shall I Mourn. Linking Education & Medicine, P.O. Box 357, Burtonsville, Maryland 20866-9357.

Surviving Abortion—Help for the Aborted Woman. Open ARMs, P.O. Box 19835, Indianapolis, Indiana 46219.

Periodicals

SET FREE. Bimonthly. Post Abortion Ministries, Inc., P.O. Box 3092, Landover Hills, Maryland 20784-0092.

APPENDIX C

Post-abortion Workbooks

Broger, John C. *Biblical Counseling Training Syllabus for Course 1: Self-confrontation.* Administrative Offices of the Biblical Counseling Foundation, 6013 Scotts Pine Court, Orlando, Florida 32819, (407) 352-7278. Twenty-four-session study; although not written specifically for aborted women, it thoroughly explains step-by-step biblical principles for change; highly recommended.

Cochrane, Linda. *Women in Ramah: A Post Abortion Bible Study.* Revised edition, PACE (Post Abortion Counseling and Education), Christian Action Council, 101 W. Broad Street, Suite 500, Falls Church, Virginia 22046, (703) 237-2100. Eight-week Bible study; to reconcile women who have had abortions to Jesus Christ through His Word.

Fangman, Terri. *Walls Evaporate, Blessings Abound Workbook.* 4900 Glenway Avenue, Cincinnati, Ohio 45238, (513) 921-9322. Seven-week study with audiotapes; pro-healing program based on reconciliation with God and self.

Freeman, Ken. *Healing Hurts of Abortion.* Last Harvest Ministries, Inc., 5477 Glen Lakes Drive, Suite 207, Dallas, Texas 75231, (800) 422-4542. Ten-week Bible study with videotapes; designed to familiarize people suffering from abortion's aftermath with God's redemptive process as it applies to their lives.

Marshall, Debbie, and Goodoien, Patti. *In His Image: A Post-Abortion Bible Study.* Open ARMs, P.O. Box 19835, Indianapolis, Indiana 46219, (317) 359-9950. Seven-week Bible study; an in-depth look into the character of God (mercy, love, etc.) as demonstrated in His interaction with people; helps people to know the God Who forgives and heals.

ABOUT THE AUTHOR

Pam Koerbel was an unmarried junior in college when she became pregnant and chose abortion in her twenty-third week of pregnancy. Pam traveled the road of denial, guilt, anger, depression, and attempted suicide until she reached the end of herself and found forgiveness and acceptance. That journey took fourteen years.

Today Pam is a wife and mother of four living children. She is frequently invited to share her personal story of victory and insights into post-abortion trauma at banquets, seminars, and media interviews.

Pam is co-founder and Ministries Coordinator of Post Abortion Ministries, Inc. She also serves on the advisory boards of pro-life and post-abortion groups in the United States and Canada.

Does Anyone Else Feel Like I Do? is her second book addressing the issue of post-abortion trauma.